# Banking on Deception

# Banking on Deception

## The Discourse of Fiscal Crisis

*Thom Workman*

Fernwood Publishing
Halifax

Editing: Anne Webb
Cover photos: Beverly Briden
Design and production: Beverley Rach
Printed and bound in Canada by: Hignell Printing Limited


A publication of:
Fernwood Publishing
Box 9409, Station A
Halifax, Nova Scotia
B3K 5S3

Fernwood Publishing Company Limited gratefully acknowledges the financial
support of The Ministry of Canadian Heritage and the Canada/Nova Scotia
Cooperation Agreement on Cultural Development.


**Canadian Cataloguing in Publication Data**
Workman, W. Thom, 1959—
Banking on Deception
(Basics from Fernwood Publishing)

Includes bibliographical references.
ISBN 1 895686 62 8

1. Debts, Public -- Canada. 2. Budget deficits -- Canada.
3. Government spending policy -- Canada. 4. Fiscal policy -- Canada.
I. Title. II. Series.

HJ8033.C3W67 1996    336.3'4'0971   C95-950335-8

# CONTENTS

# DEDICATION

To Beverly with love

# ACKNOWLEDGEMENTS

This study emerged out of an informal discussion with Garry Allen during a boating trip along the Saint John River in the fall of 1994. Many of these ideas were presented at a conference in Boston the next spring. Along the way, Garry offered invaluable encouragement that helped see the project through to completion. I wish to express my gratitude to David Bedford, who scrupulously read this manuscript and offered critical support and feedback that greatly exceed the call of camaraderie. The department of political science at the University of New Brunswick provided support for parts of this study. I am particularly grateful to Rheta Macelwain and Debbie Sloan for patiently responding to my innumerable queries and requests along the way. My thanks are also extended to Danielle Irving, a graduate student at UNB, for her help during the editing of the manuscript. I wish also to extend my gratitude to Anne Webb at Fernwood for her input and contributions to this study. Finally, for her support and careful reading of this manuscript, I lovingly thank Beverly and, in a way that perhaps only a parent could understand, Meredith, Bronwyn and Tristan.

Fredericton, NB
Spring 1996

## INTRODUCTION
# THE LORE OF DEBT CRISIS

O ver the last decade a story has emerged about Canada's debt. It may be heard again and again on the television, on the radio, in the newspapers, and in speeches by government and business leaders. According to this story, the size of the debt has reached alarming proportions. The debt is well past the one-half trillion dollar mark, and thus threatens the viability of Canada's financial and economic system. Something must be done immediately. Large yearly deficits created by careless and wasteful governments are responsible for Canada's debt, and the pattern has continued unabated for more than twenty-five years. It is an irresponsible practice that must stop. The growth of the debt must be slowed and then the debt itself reduced.

The story claims that governments must have the courage to make unpopular decisions to cut spending. Sacrifices must be made in the interest of sound fiscal management. These sacrifices, moreover, must not come through higher levels of taxation. Canada is an "over-taxed" nation. The people are tired of supporting government inefficiency out of their own pockets. Greater control and restraint must be exercised by Canada's elected leaders who, in the past, often have increased spending merely to pander to the masses. Furthermore, incumbent governments understand the electoral risks associated with reduced government spending and have been very reluctant to initiate meaningful cuts. The debt is not really a debt of necessity; it is a debt of irresponsibility and weakness. Politicians spend wildly. They are profligates. The debt has continued to grow because of the lack of political will and, perhaps more than anything else, because Canadian governments have lacked integrity.

Slowly, very slowly, political leaders have begun to recognize that government spending must be brought under control. This awareness, the story continues, has developed largely as a response to growing national and international criticism. On the domestic level, business magnates have led the call for balanced budgets. In the last decade, research centres such as the C.D. Howe Institute in Toronto or the Fraser Institute in Vancouver have focused their attention increasingly upon the debt. The editorial preoccupation of Canada's major newspapers has gradually shifted from Third World debt in the mid-1980s to Canada's home-grown debt in the mid-1990s. Over the same period, international credit rating agencies and organizations such as the International Monetary Fund have added their voices to the growing chorus of concern about Canada's debt. The common sentiment is that the growth of the debt must be reversed.

Political leaders have taken up this challenge. Budget addresses are now permeated with protestations of fiscal responsibility and discipline. Each budget is preceded by copious warnings about the dire state of Canada's finances. Finance ministers spend their pre-budget days both preparing Canadians for a new round of budget slashes and reassuring the national and international financial communities that the upcoming budget will be fiscally responsible. The profile of the finance minister's portfolio at both the provincial and federal levels has risen considerably by virtue of this process. It contains many unassailable "truths." The debt is dangerous. Governments have over-spent. Some political leaders are more courageous than others. Governments must reduce spending. People must be willing to make sacrifices. Responsibility is painful. Taxes should not be raised, and so on. The debt story is also logical. If government spending is the cause of the problem, more or less, then government spending should be cut and, if necessary, cut drastically. It is here that the courage is required. Political leaders must be prepared to make tough and often unpopular decisions to slash spending if the debt problem is to be solved. Canada faces a fiscal crisis, and only clear-headed determination to balance budgets will get the country out of its debt morass. And so crown corporations are privatized, social programs are cut and tightened, hospitals are closed, government is "downsized" and streamlined, federal-provincial fiscal arrangements are altered, special government accounts are opened up for those who wish to make one-time contributions to pay down the debt, lotteries are expanded and so forth, all with the explicit goal of saving money.

This is the lore of Canada's debt that has gained popularity. There is another interpretation of Canada's debt that directly challenges the predominant story. It appears with much less regularity. It sometimes constitutes the subject matter of newspaper columns. It may be found occasionally in the publications of groups critical of government policy. At least once, in Linda MacQuaig's *Shooting the Hippo*, it formed the subject matter of an entire book. A few politicians articulate some of the ideas of this other story, as do labour unions and some women's groups. Although not often, it has appeared in official government publications. Of course, there are some places where it is never found. It does not appear in the declarations of finance ministers or in mainstream newspaper editorials. It does not guide newscasts or journalistic commentaries in the dominant media. Business groups do not voice it. Put rather bluntly, it is rarely the starting point for political commentary anywhere in the country.

Of course, the less popular debt story is very different. The cause of the debt, for instance, has little or nothing to do with government spending. The very notion of government over-spending is attacked as a myth. The debt is blamed, instead, on corporate tax breaks and the maintenance of inflation-fighting high interest rates by the Bank of Canada, a practice that greatly increases interest payments on the debt. And the idea that there is a crisis is challenged directly. The Canadian Centre for Policy Alternative's "The Deficit Made Me Do It!: The Myths about Government Debt" (Chorney, Hotson and Seccareccia 1992) claims the notion of a debt crisis is a convenient tool for those in power: "Governments these days find it easy to defend cuts in services and programs. All they have to do is point to their annual deficits and their total accumulated debts. . . . 'We're broke,' they tell us plaintively. 'We can't afford to increase public services, or even keep them at their present level.'"

Critical speculation about the motives of political and business leaders is sometimes expressed openly. A 17 June 1995 column by Thomas Walkom in the *Toronto Star* compares the deficit concerns of the Harris government in Ontario and the Liberal government in Ottawa. Walkom accuses business leaders and politicians of fabricating the debt crisis in order to lower labour costs: ". . . the forces behind Harris—the business elite, the financial house, the sophisticated right—don't care that much about deficits . . . . They say they do. They've managed to convince much of the public that deficits are the major threat to Canadian society. But they themselves are not bothered to excess by government debt. They care far more about other things. They want cutbacks to those elements of social spending that support wages, such as welfare and unemployment insurance. That's simply because they want to keep wage costs down." The point that, for the most part, business is not highly concerned about government debts and deficits is illustrated by events which surrounded the federal budget earlier in the year.

> During the weeks leading up to the Martin budget, the financial
> houses were in a panic. Martin had to make deep spending cuts in
> order to bring the deficit down, it was said, or else the New York
> bond rating agencies would downgrade Canada's debt. . . . Even-
> tually, Martin brought down his budget. It didn't solve the debt
> problem. In fact, one New York bond rating agency, Moody's, did

downgrade Canada's credit rating for that very reason. But Moody's action was a non-event. Business didn't care. Because while Martin has not fundamentally addressed the deficit issue, he had done what business really wanted: cut social spending without raising taxes. (ibid.)

And, Walkom concludes, the newly elected Harris government in Ontario will conduct itself similarly: "So it will be with Mike Harris. The people from Moody's may indeed come calling. They may even downgrade Ontario's credit rating if his tax cuts interfere with deficit reduction. In the Legislature, New Democrats will harangue Harris for being fiscally irresponsible and grind their teeth in frustration. But it won't matter to him or to those who back him. Because it never really did (ibid.)."

And thus there are at least two stories about Canada's debt. These two stories have profoundly different plot lines. One is heard widely and understood by most, while the other is rarely heard. One emphasizes fiscal crisis linked to government over-spending. The other denies that there is a fiscal crisis, and emphasizes corporate coddling by the government and the Bank of Canada's tight monetary policies. One holds that living with debt is dangerous for a country. The other contends that claims about impending fiscal doom are being used to justify rolling back government. Living with debt is no cause to be alarmed, according to the latter view.

Only the former story has entered the popular imagination of Canadians. Indeed, it is so widely understood that finance ministers no longer have to articulate it: "The last thing Canadians need," Paul Martin correctly declared in his 1995 budget address, "is another lecture on the danger of the deficit." Martin could readily identify the debt problem as a critical element in the development and justification of Liberal policy: "Not to act now to put our fiscal house in order would be to abandon the purposes for which our Party exists and this government stands—competence, compassion, reform and hope." As he concluded his budget address Martin equated his attack on the federal deficit with the forging of a stronger country: "Canadians can have confidence now in a country that has put the era of band-aid budgets behind it. . . . We have made our choice—against the status quo and in favour of a stronger country." It is important to note that nowhere in Martin's 1995 budget speech, a speech justifying policies almost exclusively in terms of deficit reduction, did he explain the exact contours and nature of the fiscal threat looming over the country. The threat, he safely assumed, was taken by the public to be real.

Why has one debt story gained the status of unquestioned truth while the other has gained little or no popular support? It is the working position of this book that the second debt story—the story that is not part of our day-to-day understanding—is much more accurate. And thus our question becomes: "Why is the highly dubious debt story so well received?" Conversely: "Why is the historically correct understanding of the debt not part of our everyday consciousness?"

This study provides an answer to these questions. It offers an explanation as to why the widely believed debt story has rooted itself in the popular understanding of Canadians. This explanation focuses upon the relationship between different elements of the widely circulated debt story on one side, and popular understandings and ideas—the world of common sense—on the other. It argues that the prevailing debt story—more formally identified as the *discourse of fiscal crisis* in this study—draws upon notions and ideas embedded in everyday life. Rather than challenging day-to-day intuitions, it is assisted by them. More specifically, the story tends to be framed in a way that is informed by elementary cultural notions inherent to Western history, patriarchal consciousness and ideas about financial self-reliance. Therefore, it is believable, agreeable and convincing. In the end, the popular version of the debt crisis appears infinitely reasonable to most Canadians.

The implications of the popular debt story are socially pernicious. Greater and greater segments of society become pauperized while the "Lazarus-layers" of the working classes spiral downwards. The idea of fiscal crisis has allowed successive governments to continually reduce the role of the state in the economy and in social life. It has catalyzed that basket of policies—including deregulation, welfare reformism and privitization—commonly referred to as neo-liberalism. In other words, the widespread support for neo-liberal policies, even among elements of the dispossessed classes, is owing to the ease with which the discourse of fiscal crisis has affixed itself to Canadian political life. Essentially, the prevailing debt narrative tells us that a state that is broke should get out of the economy (a basic feature of neo-liberalism).

The discourse of fiscal crisis serves the super-corporations (and tends as well to be not all that unkind to smaller capital) by legitimizing policies conducive to their accumulation strategies, and by aiding significantly in the restructuring of class relations. It is with this restructuring that this study begins. Declining levels of profitability after the late 1960s resulted in efforts to restore profitability. Predictably, capital strategized that this restoration would be achieved by lowering production costs through i) restructuring production and ii) by attempting to lower wages. Both of these efforts have led capital to take advantage of its always-increasing mobility, which forces all nation states into heightened competition to lure capital investment or retard capital flight. For each state, successful capitalist development is contingent upon its ability to offer attractive business environments. The principles of neo-liberalism have gained a great deal of currency in this regard, especially those principles that effectively condition labour markets by removing income supports. When necessary, international disciplining institutions such as the International Monetary Fund or the World Bank ensure the adoption of neo-liberal policies, often by requiring adoption of the former's structural adjustment programs.

Of course, implementing these policies can require copious amounts of brute force, as the situation in Mexico following the adoption of the North American Free Trade Agreement so clearly demonstrates. Nonetheless, in some countries, such as France and Canada, the popularized discourse of fiscal crisis has convinced the population of the need to support neo-liberal policies that favour capitalist investment. The restructuring of class relations implied by the adoption of neo-liberal policies has been abetted by the salient social conviction that the state is broke. Working-class opposition to harmful neo-liberal policies is thwarted by the belief that the state is in financial crisis. Put another way, a renewed and reworked class hegemony which rests upon diminished hopes and blunted aspirations of the working and marginalized classes is being forged. Alienated and impoverished people hesitatingly support (neo-liberal) policies that intensify their alienation and poverty, at least in the short run. This needs to be explained. By exploring the underlying cultural factors that lend credibility to the prevailing debt story, I hope that this brief study, in tandem with the efforts of many others, can tease out the disquiet that is already evident. The class struggle is out of sight, but it has not vanished.

The remaining chapters explore the consonance between the discourse of fiscal crisis and a wider culture background. Chapter three explores the debt discourse in terms of the prevailing linear narrative of history, and calls attention to the sense of historical decay and the manner in which history is metaphorically presented through images of bodily illness and wellness. Chapter four discusses the links between the discourse and gendered life, focusing in particular upon the ideas of courage and bravery, concerns about control, representations of the economy and fiscal policy in the abstract, the association of the debt discourse with reason and reasonableness, and the voice of authority. Chapter five looks at the debt discourse in the context of the culture of self-reliance, especially the common analogy to personal finances.

CHAPTER ONE

# GLOBALIZATION AND THE DEVELOPMENT OF NEO-LIBERALISM

C anadian society is in the midst of a marked ideological shift. The spectrum of political debate in Canada has narrowed and simultaneously glided rapidly to the right. The classical left-centre-right ideological pivot characteristic of the post- Second World War era, to the extent that it identified different policy baskets, has disintegrated. Canadian political life now rotates on a new axis. Policy options taken seriously as little as a decade ago, especially regarding the expansion or implementation of social programs such as a national daycare system, are no longer considered seriously by governments. The ideological core of Canadian society—a menu of policy choices forever mindful of power and widely intuited as sensible and reasonable—has evolved in the context of a new age.

Of course, this shift is mystified. Canadians are reminded repeatedly that they have entered a new era of pragmatism. The end of the Cold War dramatically confirms that the age of ideology is over. We have optimistically assigned ourselves to a new era of globalization. Outmoded ideological intransigence will only land us in trouble. This is no time for fossilized politics. A new sensitivity to global constraints and vulnerabilities must replace antiquated ideological battles. *Dogmaticus Rex* must be put to sleep.

Despite these protestations, the end of ideology is not quite with us. Rather, this aforementioned shift represents the consolidation of neo-liberalism. Ironically, and illustrative of the breakdown of the left-centre-right ideological spectrum, the new orthodoxy is sometimes called neo-conservativism. Regardless of its label, this ascendent ideology is, at root, a radical distillation of free market thinking essentially in the service of lower production costs, especially lower wages. It is attended by an ideology of ridicule. Neo-liberalism has evolved quickly to attack the poor rather than poverty, workers instead of the nature of their work, "criminals" rather than "crime," racial groups rather than racism, women rather than patriarchy, the sick, the physically challenged, the psychologically distressed, and so on. The new distemper is fundamentally punitive as well. It opts for increasing the daily hardship of many of the most vulnerable segments of society, enlisting a dazzling array of justifying shibboleths. And it is reversional. It seeks to roll back the hard fought gains of previous generations, especially those of the working class. This new ideological atmosphere is thoroughly reactionary. As its tragic human consequences increase it continues to engender well-honed hatist backlashes that routinely surface in all manner of popular dialogue.

As yet, curiously, there is very little in the way of broad-based opposition to neo-liberal policies. Instances of resistance can certainly be found. In August 1995, the Catholic Bishops of Ontario sent a letter to newly-elected premier Mike Harris urging him to avoid solving the province's fiscal problems on the backs of the poor. The letter, released just as the Harris government forced cuts in the Toronto Transit Commission's services for disabled people, was in response to a series of initiatives by the Harris government that clearly increased the hardship of the poor in Ontario. "We cannot allow an undue burden to fall on the poor, the unemployed, the marginalized, the young or the challenged," the letter stressed, "nor can we deprive any person or groups of the basic right to share in the wealth of the province." In another example, in late April 1994, a group of angry construction workers stormed the Nova Scotia legislature to protest against a government decision to allow non-unionized scab workers onto construction sites. The premier of the province, John Savage, was among a group of politicians kicked and punched in the ensuing scuffle. The speaker of the Nova Scotia legislature cancelled the session for the day, thereby forcing the finance minister to deliver his budget to the house clerk. In June 1995, a group of women organized by the Quebec Women's Federation marched from Montreal to Quebec City to protest against the growing number of women living in poverty. About one thousand women walked the entire distance over a ten-day period. They were joined by more than twelve thousand additional women as they approached the National Assembly in Quebec City. The women demanded that Quebec's minimum wage be raised to $8.00 per hour from its rate of $6.00 per hour. The rally prompted the appearance of government ministers, including the employment minister

Louise Harel. Harel was booed strongly when she announced that the government was raising the minimum wage to $6.45 per hour.

Thus resistance to neo-liberal policies is fragmented and sporadic. Critical commentary is sustained by some constituencies typically at odds with government policies in Canada. Labour groups hasten to emphasize the harmful nature of the last two decades upon their members. Women's groups, such as the National Action Committee on the Status of Women, consistently call attention to the adverse effects of recent policies upon women in Canadian society. However, no visible broad-based struggle against the neo-liberal program has formed, let alone had an impact.

This study offers one explanation for the curious lack of co-ordinated mass opposition to policy shifts that extract such heavy human tolls. I begin by noting that the prevailing public discourse regarding Canada's debt has made neo-liberal policy appear to be the only reasonable option for government. We are told that a state that is broke, a state that cannot afford to be *in* the economy, should *get out* of the economy. Thus, the current debt discourse opens the door for the wholesale introduction of the neo-liberal agenda, especially its emphasis on privatization, de-regulation and the rolling back of welfare programs.

The primary task of this study is to explore the source of the persuasive power of the dominant debt discourse. I argue that the prevailing representation of the debt holds sway in large measure because it resonates positively within a foundational cultural canvas. It fits well with "common" sense. In effect, the prevailing debt discourse makes sense by drawing upon, rather than confronting, everyday common understandings. My overall argument can be summarized as follows:

- the concern around government fiscal policy and the debt has coalesced into a relatively coherent set of ideas referred to in this study as *the discourse of fiscal crisis*. This debt discourse offers a particular account of the debt and a singular solution to the debt crisis, a solution that largely involves a roll-back of the Keynesian welfare state;
- the discourse of fiscal crisis has become the predominant discourse around the debt in part because of its consonance with a wider cultural or intersubjective cloth;
- the hegemonic debt discourse has come to provide a powerful rationale for the introduction of neo-liberal policies, a rationale that is widely accepted across class lines. In other words, the discourse of fiscal crisis is integral to the creation of a consensual base for neo-liberalism.

The remainder of this chapter provides the setting for this study. My first objective is to establish the global context for the changes afoot in

Canadian society. The evolution of the international economy has figured prominently in the shift in governing approaches in Canada. The shift can be described as the break-down of the Keynesian governing consensus and the rise of neo-liberal orthodoxy. This chapter outlines these processes in four parts:

- the shifting global context is reviewed by calling attention to the crisis of corporate profitability that began to emerge in the late 1960s. This crisis was followed by the appearance of generalized global economic disruptions during the 1970s;
- stress the fact that the Canadian response to the global economic disruptions cannot be separated from the struggle among contending social forces domestically. In other words, I take care not to reify the global economy. I pay specific attention to the role of the Business Council on National Issues (BCNI);
- the evolution of this struggle among classes in Canada, which features an aggressive attack by capital upon many elements of the post-Second World War class compromise, undergirds the erosion of the Keynesian consensus and the rise of the neo-liberal orthodoxy;
- the discourse of fiscal crisis enters directly into this struggle. That is, the debt discourse has been enlisted to defend neo-liberal orthodoxy, especially to the extent that the discourse advances solutions consistent with the neo-liberal agenda.

The remaining chapters of the study explore those factors that account for the persuasive power of the discourse of fiscal crisis.

## The Fordist Transition

An analysis of the evolution of Canadian politics needs to be situated within the context of the changing global economy. The global economy has been undergoing fundamental changes since the early 1970s. It has been experiencing protracted difficulties, and subsequently taken on a significantly altered form. The most visible manifestations of these problems in the early 1970s included successive bouts of inflation, high levels of unemployment, underutilization of economic capacity (this was especially pronounced in some sectors of the economy, such as manufacturing) and relatively low rates of economic growth. The emerging crisis of the early 1970s became evident with the 1971 collapse of the Bretton Woods Agreement that fixed exchange rates to the US dollar and the dollar, in turn, to gold. The oil price shocks of 1973 also figured prominently in the West. Higher levels of unemployment combined with high levels of inflation persisted throughout the 1970s.

The root of these problems lay in the myriad of responses by individual corporations and co-ordinating bodies to falling levels of profitability. High levels of profitability in the immediate post-Second World War period continued for two decades. However, in the late 1960s, the higher profit levels characteristic of the 1950s and early 1960s evaporated rather quickly, giving way to a period of "unprecedented weak profitability" (Duménil, Glick and Rangel 1985: 139).

These declines triggered the search to restore pre-1970s rates of profitability. Effectively, the falling rates of profitability initiated the capitalist restructuring that has characterized the last two decades. In an important sense, the range of opportunities for capital were limited owing to heightened international competition (which reduces the ability to raise prices) and a relatively institutionalized system in the North of wage determination (which would minimize the easy slashing of wage levels) (Cox 1987: 275–308). Inevitably, efforts to increase profitability ran headlong into what have been called Fordist institutions and practices.[1] Fordism is based on the practice of mass production for mass consumption. In a broader sense, Fordism encompasses a specific scheme of capitalist production (a regime of accumulation focusing upon economies of scale) and the widely accepted social and political practices attendant to that scheme (the mode of regulation with entrenched systems of wage determination and the Keynesian welfare state). Fordist arrangements came to be seen as inhibiting capitalist restructuring, especially with respect to their perceived "inflexibilities" in the areas of production (exploiting economies of scale), wage determination and labour markets. As a result, Fordist practices have entered a period of sustained disintegration or decomposition. Efforts to sustain profitability have resulted in a definite move away from Fordist practices, and the nation-state has been universally enlisted in this process by capital.

It is helpful to observe that Fordism emerged as a model of production that was specific to the United States in the early part of the twentieth century, and subsequently expanded globally. It was the product of both prolonged struggles waged by the working class and reluctant concessions made by capital. Fordism is best understood as a class compromise. Workers reluctantly submitted to certain principles of production (including Taylorism)[2] in exchange for a wage that allowed for mass consumption. In other words, a mass market was effectively created for capitalists intent on exploiting new production technologies and the innovative organization of the shop floor. Keynesian principles emerged in the context of this compromise to smooth out economic cycles.[3] State welfare became a register of hard fought working class victories. Effectively, the state emerged as an economic "backstop" to the Fordist class settlements. Due to its balancing of production and consumption, Fordism is often credited with stabilizing capitalism throughout much of the twentieth century.

The contemporary post-Fordist regime which is replacing Fordism has been characterized in various ways. It is described as the development of a core-peripheral model of production (Cox 1987), a disorganized model of production (Lash and Urry 1987), and a flexible model of accumulation (Harvey 1989). In effect, Fordist principles and practices, which are no longer viewed as optimally conducive to accumulation, are being abandoned in favour of much more limited economies of scale. The new arrangements focus on greater flexibility in production and labour markets. On the side of production, there are rapid infusions of technology into the production process, a cultivation of a sort of lying-in-wait preparedness with respect to market demand (especially with the expansion of last-minute or just-in-time production schemes), informal production by stealth, the introduction of greater product ranges and small-batch production. Greater flexibility in production has been complemented by an effort to force labour responsiveness by attacking trade unions, weakening state labour supports, hiring illegal workers and migrant workers, and by off-loading labour costs through contracting out, job sharing, workplace rationalization and streamlining, and the expansion of part-time work.

This transition away from the increasingly obsolete Fordist model (obsolete in the sense that Fordist practices were ill-suited for accumulation strategies after the late 1960s), particularly the subsequent search for cheaper labour costs, has intensified the globalization of production. During this transitional period there has been an increase in the transnational nature of financial capital. The growing dynamics of the international economy, combined with the increasing ease of rapid movements of financial capital, investment strikes and capital flight, have heightened awareness about the vulnerability of domestic economies to extraneous factors. As a result, there is a growing sense of domestic economic insecurity in this era of rapid change and intensified globalization. Neither national economies nor individual corporations can be insulated from global developments. A new era of vulnerability is understood to have arrived. State policy makers must look inwards and outwards. National economic policies must be developed with a view to the reaction of local *and* international capital. Increasingly, there is the view that national economic policy must be subordinated to the exigencies of the global economy. In the last two decades, "states became more effectively accountable to a *nébuleuse* personified as the global economy; and they were constrained to mystify this external accountability in the eyes and ears of their own publics through the new vocabulary of globalization, interdependence, and competitiveness" (Cox 1992: 27).

## The Evolution of Fordism and the Transitional State

The changing role of the state is the subject of much controversy in analyses of the global economy. It is often recognized that specific state forms (e.g., authoritarian-military or liberal democracy) are most appropriate to different locations and periods of globalization (for example, see Jessop's discussion, 1993). Similarly, it has been observed that the state has become increasingly internationalized; significant elements of the state are involved in the process of co-ordinating or calibrating domestic policies with the policies of international organizations and market disciplining elements. These observations suggest that the state is more or less a derivative phenomenon and, taking the situation in Europe into consideration, that we might be witnessing the final stages of the modern capitalist state. The processes of economic globalization, if not entirely supplanting the state, are at least causing its function and nature to change profoundly according to some analysts.

Such claims are greatly exaggerated, however, and run the risk of obfuscating the integral role of the state in global economic developments. Globalization has yet to lash back very hard against states. It is not so much that the process of globalization causes nation state level changes, but that the evolution of states has prompted so-called global developments. As hegemonic constellations among states evolve and reconstitute themselves, developments at the global level are prompted and encouraged. Change in the hegemonic configuration of states is a cause of globalization rather than an outcome. The dynamics of global social forces or the development of a supra-national intersubjectivity have affected struggles at the domestic level but are far from eclipsing them.

In this sense, the contemporary terminology, replete with references to globalizing processes and restructuring, contributes to the process of hegemonic reproduction. Globalization becomes less of a process and more of a catch-all phrase routinely invoked to justify or legitimize the hegemonic re-configuration of states. Canadian society has not simply been calibrated with global economic necessities; co-ordinating domestic and international economies is a politically loaded affair, not merely the logistical side of more geographically vast developments. As Panitch has written, "capitalist globalization is a process which also takes place in, through, and under the aegis of states; it is encoded by them and in important respects even authored by them; and it involves a shift in power relations within states that often means the centralisation and concentration of state power as the necessary condition of and accompaniment to global market discipline" (1994: 64) Thus, we must avoid the error of determining "the internal evolution of each national social formation as though it were *a partita* executed under the direction of a global maestro" (Lipietz 1986: 17).

Explicit recognition of the continuing pivotal role of state-level struggles in contemporary economic processes helps to shed light upon the
apparent calibration of Canadian society with the forces of globalization. In
effect, the co-ordination of the Canadian state with the global economy is
largely the product of the deeper, more salient role that domestic social
forces—forces that are wrapped up with the Fordist transition globally—
have come to play in the formation of Canadian public policy. Specifically,
large multinational corporations have ensconced themselves at the apex of
the effective political hierarchy. Although their influence has always been
significant, there are strong indications that it has increased dramatically
over the last two decades. The most visible manifestation of this phenomenon in Canada is the Business Council on National Issues (BCNI), although
large corporations are also often highly visible in terms of their sectoral
lobbies, such as in pharmaceuticals. The BCNI, composed of the one hundred
and fifty or so most profitable corporations in Canada, was formed in the
mid-1970s. The BCNI was formed ostensibly to respond to the lack of a
coherent corporate voice in the political process. More accurately, however,
it has formulated policies consistent with the giant multinational corporations' accumulation strategies during the twilight of Fordism. Through the
1980s, especially with the election of the Mulroney government, the impact
of the BCNI on government policy increased measurably (see Langille 1987).
The policy agenda of the BCNI, especially regarding state regulation and open
trade, were adopted by the Mulroney government. All the theoretical
wincing in the world cannot hide the fact that a sort of crude instrumentalism
between large capital and the state has ruled in Canada for the last decade.

The growing salience of large capital (over medium and small capital)
is complemented by the growing presence of business-funded organizations. In particular, the Vancouver-based Fraser Institute and the Toronto-
based C.D. Howe Institute (named after an unrelenting free-market apolo-
gist from the early post-Second World War period) have acquired an
authoritative and almost unassailable status. Historically, the policy orientation of the Fraser Institute was much more pro-business and market
oriented than the C.D. Howe. However, during the 1980s, a purer neo-liberal
policy orientation emerged at the latter institute (see Ernst 1992). The C.D.
Howe became a staunch supporter of free trade in the 1980s and began to
work much more closely with the Mulroney regime. More recently, the C.D.
Howe Institute has become a key commentator on Canada's debt.

Despite the fact that the C.D. Howe and Fraser Institutes are funded
almost exclusively by business, and notwithstanding the fact that their
policy orientations are unapologetically pro-capital, they are often identified by the media as non-partisan and independent. Their reports and policy
commentaries typically receive wide media coverage. Fraser and C.D.

Howe studies on free trade, taxation policy, government corporations, fiscal policy, federal and provincial budgets, government debt, and numerous other economic and political topics are circulated widely. It was perfectly appropriate that Eric Malling, host of CTV's flagship news program *W5*, cited the C.D. Howe Institute as his "best source for economic information—not just for facts, but perspective," a quote that was proudly displayed on the front cover of the institute's annual report in 1992.

## Post-Fordism and the Shifting Norms of Governance

What have these changes meant for Canada? Essentially, the evolution of Canadian politics in the context of the decline of Fordism has resulted in a fundamental shift in the norms of government. This shift can be summarized as a breakdown of the Keynesian political consensus beginning in the 1970s and the emergence of a neo-liberal orthodoxy during the 1980s. The new set of governing principles began to take shape with the deepening global economic difficulties. Grant Reuber, an adviser to the Conservative government in 1979 and former senior vice-president and chief economist with the Bank of Montreal, argued in the 1970s, for example, that any response to the economic difficulties in Canada would require a substantially reinforced business-friendly orientation. According to Reuber, "For the business sector this means the acceptance of high profits for those enterprises that are capable of coping effectively with international competition as well as the acceptance of business losses and bankruptcies for those enterprises that cannot. For labour it means accepting a standard of living that corresponds with productivity in relation to that of major competitors abroad. And for government it means policies that are consistent with Canada's international competitive position" (Reuber 1980: 126).

Throughout the 1970s and the early 1980s, the ideas summarized by Reuber caught on. The initiative for change, however, came primarily from the big business community. As Michael Ornstein, on the basis of a series of interviews with business, labour and political elites, pointed out, the ideology of big business involves strong opposition to increasing the power of trade unions and direct state investment in the economy, and weaker opposition to the co-optation of labour. It also involves support for foreign investment, economic continentalism, fiscal conservatism and a significant rejection of social welfare. In general, big business favours keeping conservative parties committed to a capitalist agenda in power in national politics (Ornstein 1985: 151).

By the mid-1980s, especially with the election of the Mulroney government in 1984 and the release of the MacDonald Commission studies on Canadian politics and society in 1985, the outline of the neo-liberal agenda was clear. Central to neo-liberalism is an unyielding faith in the performance of so-called free markets. In its broadest sense, the "free market" refers to the relatively unfettered allocation of capital and labour according to rudimentary supply and demand dynamics. Contemporary proponents of the free market adopt a utilitarian posture by emphasizing that free markets yield the greatest social good. While most proponents of free markets would accept that markets can create problems or difficulties, on the whole they believe that the social and political gains far outweigh the costs.

From this basic unrelenting commitment to a free market springs a number of specific practices and policy dimensions most characteristic of neo-liberalism. Generally, these informal practices and promulgated policies are aimed at creating environments conducive to profitability by reducing the "drag" on business operations. On a worldwide scale there is the intensified development of areas of relatively unfettered economic activity, sometimes called export processing zones. In these areas states will clear and expropriate land (often Aboriginal lands), insure that environmental regulations are relaxed, insure that labour legislation remains poor and ineffective, develop the economic infrastructure and make generous tax concessions. There are clear signs that zones extremely conducive to businesses are being created in Canada. In the province of New Brunswick, for example, the state aggressively sponsors the development of the electronic service industry, creating a sort of service processing zone. It provides tax incentives (New Brunswick waives sales tax on all 1-800 calls and provides additional tax incentives to companies), promotes infrastructural development (especially its high-tech fibre optic telephone system of NB-Tel), builds on a very close relationship between capital and the state, seizes upon its bi-lingual workforce, ensures that labour legislation remains undeveloped and relatively ineffectual, advertises its low wage levels (euphemistically called a low cost-of-living), and ensures the presence of a "flexible" labour market by combining generalized poverty and recent government attacks on social programs. It is significant that the province is often viewed as a laboratory for the rest of Canada. Indeed, other Canadian provinces have taken to declaring that they also are "open for business," an expression summarizing a willingness to gravitate rapidly towards an even more business-friendly (neo-liberal) model of economic growth.

In Canada, the introduction of neo-liberal policies received a boost with the implementation of the Free Trade Agreement (FTA) with the United States, and later the North American Free Trade Agreement (NAFTA) between Mexico, Canada and the United States. As two commentators have recently argued, these policies act as a "restructuring tool or, put differently, as a conditioning institutional framework that promotes and consolidates neo-liberal restructuring" (Grinspun and Kreklewich 1994: 33). Thus, free trade agreements such as the FTA and NAFTA emerged within the context of neo-liberalism and at the same time further the neo-liberal agenda.

There are a number of specific policies that constitute a neo-liberal agenda, all of which relate to the basic emphasis on free markets. In particular, state activity has come to be viewed as an inhibitor to the development of free markets. There has been a marked cultivation of a *state-out orientation*. The state is something that has come to be seen as "being in the way" of routine economic practice. The counter-cyclical back-stopping state of the Keynesian era has been repudiated in favour of the state-as-a-mere-accessory-to-accumulation orientation of neo-liberalism. In effect, the activities of the state in the past have become the burden of business in the present.

A clear instance of this state-out orientation may be found in the growing calls for deregulation. Regulation serves the crucial function of co-ordinating the economic system in its entirety. State sanctioned rules of conduct create order and predictability in the conduct of individual businesses. In the last two decades, however, regulation has increasingly come to be viewed more and more as an obstruction to businesses, especially the regulation of specific industries. Paul Martin's remarks in his 1994 budget address were telling, but not at all unique: "What they [small business] do need is a government that gets off their backs, and stops burdening them with unnecessary regulations and red tape" (1994: 4).

There is also a clear push towards the privatization or dissolution of state corporations. This push is spurred by the attitude that government tends to "do" business very poorly and inefficiently. In Canada, the federal and provincial governments are off-loading crown corporations with an alacrity unmatched in the past. Privatization is effectively a delivery of economic assets to the private sector through direct sale. As the federal government declared in its 1995 budgetary address, "our view is straightforward. If government doesn't *need* to run something, it *shouldn't*. And in the future, it *won't*" (27 February 1995: 14, original emphasis). Between 1984 and 1993 the federal government in Canada privatized or dissolved thirty-nine crown corporations.

The "downsizing" and streamlining of the government and government programs are integral features of neo-liberalism. Again, the idea that government is "in the way" or "less qualified" to be involved in the economy underlines this view. The idea of downsizing government has become the cornerstone of government policies throughout Canada, and was most evident in 1995 with the announcement that the federal civil service would be reduced by forty-five thousand jobs. At the same time, social assistance programs are being constantly scaled back or cut entirely. Eligibility requirements are being tightened with the erosion of universality or the introduction of workfare schemes. Assistance levels are lowered through cuts and by failing to keep pace with levels of inflation, and the scope of coverage (especially in the area of health care) is being narrowed.

Other policies such as shifting tax burdens away from corporations and an aggressive attack upon labour unions and labour legislation round out the neo-liberal policy basket. Neo-liberalism, in summary, is designed to optimize the conditions of capital accumulation as individual corporations confront the perceived rigidities of Fordism. In many areas (but certainly not all) the state has come to be seen as an obstacle or barrier to a well-functioning economy.

## Enter Fiscal Crisis

Another development occurred alongside the emerging global economic crisis of the mid-1970s. The federal government began to regularly table budgetary deficits. This was not the first time that deficit spending had been employed by the federal government. There are two earlier periods in Canadian history when yearly deficits were the norm, the most recent one being during Second World War. This deficit, however, ushered in a protracted chain of annual deficits that has remained unbroken to this day. The prevailing representation of Canada's growing debt (approaching around $600 billion officially) has served to rationalize and legitimize the adoption of neo-liberal policies. The links are most evident in budget declarations over the last decade. Invariably, neo-liberal policies are presented in the context of concern over the condition of Canadian finances. In describing the role of the state in his 1995 budget address, for example, Paul Martin stressed that the state was to provide the framework for the private sector through "responsible policies on inflation, on taxation, regulation, trade, and the labour market" (1995: 8). He then added that his government was determined to create trade opportunities for Canada in Asia and Latin America. He then immediately contextualized these ideas with reference to Canada's fiscal situation. The role of our government is "to ensure that the nation's finances are healthy. It is to do what only government can do best—and leave the rest for those who can do better—whether business, labour, or the voluntary sector." Two years earlier Martin's predecessor, Don Mazankowski, directly linked government downsizing to the condition of Canadian finances: "Like Canadian businesses, governments must reduce costs and operate more efficiently. The measures in this budget have been designed to encourage continued improvement. . . . In the eyes of the business client, a bewildering array of federal, provincial, municipal and private sector services are being offered, leaving the impression of complexity, overlap, duplication and all-around inefficiency" (1993: 11). To this end Mazankowski promised to reduce the "regulatory burden."

Take away the cultivated debt paranoia and neo-liberal policies are a tougher sell, especially the dismantling of the welfare state. What has allowed the dominant debt discourse to facilitate the introduction of neo-liberal policies? How do the ideas regarding state indebtedness catalyze and legitimize the profoundly redefined role of the state? What makes the discourse of fiscal crisis so persuasive and powerful? To answer these questions, we now turn to an analysis of the debt discourse.

## Notes

1. The term Fordism has been used to describe the aspect of twentieth century capitalism concerned with the relationship between economic production and social consumption, that is, the mass production of goods such as automobiles or appliances—what economists call *economies of scale*—and the ability of society to purchase these goods. The idea of Fordism builds upon the notion that the making of commodities requires a specific organization of society. As Gramsci wrote at the outset of the development of Fordist practices in the United States, "a long process is needed for this [the extension of Fordism], during which a change must take place in social conditions and in the way of life and the habits of individuals" (Gramsci 1971: 312).

2. The concept of Taylorism grew out of the research and writings of Frederick Winslow Taylor, especially his *The Principles of Scientific Management* (Taylor 1919). In an effort to increase productivity, Taylor divided the labour process into a series of measurable or quantifiable activities. His approach rationalized the intensification of the division of labour and helped to wrestle control of the labour process away from workers themselves. Importantly, workers initially resisted this loss of control. Such developments are highly amenable to assembly line production, and represent another step in the transformation of "working humanity" into an "instrument of capital" (Braverman 1974: 139). More generally, the concept of Taylorism draws attention to the growing alienation of workers during the twentieth century; it removed any residual worker control over the labour processes that characterized earlier periods of capitalism (for discussion of the Canadian context, see Rinehart 1987: 47–53).

3. Keynesianism refers to the application of policies propounded in the writings of John Meynard Keynes. Most importantly, it refers to the orientation of state policies (through its fiscal and monetary levers) towards the maintenance of conditions of full employment. In effect, Keynesianism gave the state a green light to intervene in the economy in order to smooth over periods of relatively slow economic growth, and provided ideological justification for the expansion of the welfare state.

## CHAPTER TWO

# CLASS RELATIONS AND THE DISCOURSE OF FISCAL CRISIS

E xtensive shifts in government policy are usually greeted with opposition from those adversely effected. The more dramatic the change the more aggressive the resistance. This is particularly true when the changes encroach upon class interests. It is one of the most curious developments in recent Canadian history, therefore, that the ascendency of the neo-liberal basket of policies, a basket that entails a profound encroachment upon the working class and the marginalized poor in Canadian society, has met with proportionately little resistance.

It is my contention that the ascendency of the neo-liberal orthodoxy has been catalyzed significantly by the discourse of fiscal crisis, that is, a post mid-1970s discursive landscape that emphasizes responsible fiscal management in the face of grave government indebtedness. The discourse begins with the idea that Canadians currently face an unwieldy public debt. The size of the debt is due to the accumulation of year-by-year deficits of spendthrift governments at the provincial and federal levels. Consequently, there is a perceived need to curb the growth of the debt and reduce it to a manageable size. Raising taxes is not an option since Canadians are "taxed out." Therefore, the goal of debt management can be achieved only by cuts in government spending. As an ultimate goal, the debt should be dramatically reduced because of the high cost of paying interest on the outstanding principal. The failure to bring the federal debt under control, according to the debt discourse, could result in a credit crisis for one or both levels of government. Such a development would result in a loss of Canada's sovereignty. That is, in view of the large number of foreign creditors or due to the potential role of global agencies such as the International Monetary Fund, the Canadian government could be forced to accede *de facto* control of its spending to outside forces.

The discourse of fiscal crisis has become as much a constitutive as strategic element in political life. It structures political thinking and is consciously employed for political gain. What might be perceived by many as opportunism, advantage, convenience or legerdemain blends imperceptibly into belief, conviction, sensibility, meaningfulness and truth. There are many blended aspects to the operation of the discourse. First, the discourse of fiscal crisis assigns seriousness and establishes concern. It identifies the debt as a matter of grave importance and as something warranting attention and respect. The dangers it poses must be borne in mind when setting public policy. The debt, according to Liberal Finance Minister Paul Martin, is a "black cloud" hanging over the Canadian political landscape. Policy agendas must be subordinated to the requirements of debt management. When talking about the debt it is appropriate to speak in ominous, foreboding or austere ways. To question the severity of the debt is to disregard irresponsibly its overwhelming threat to Canadians.

Second, the debt discourse fixes fiscal "truths" or establishes fiscal "givens." Perhaps most importantly, through constant reiteration the idea that a debt crisis even exists at all enters the social consciousness. The dangerous magnitude of the debt becomes the implicit given in all policy discussion. In other words, the primary truth that frames all debates about policy is that Canada is in the middle of a debt crisis or that such a crisis is close at hand. Further "truths" are that the source of the problem lies on the spending side of the government's fiscal equation and that Canadians are taxed to the limit. It is also understood that there is some identifiable point at which Canada's fiscal situation will reach a critical threshold, the so-called "debt wall." These givens tend to go unchallenged, and inform all subsequent discussions and practices.

Third, the discourse of fiscal crisis secures the margins of debate—what aspects deficits and the debt are talked about—through the relative weighting of subjects. One must talk about the debt only in a manner that draws attention, for example, to government expenditures, debt-servicing costs or looming tax revolts. Speaking about the debt in terms of the super-corporate agenda, the class struggle, the backlash against women, the created need for but absence of access to baby formulae or inherent ethical problems with capitalism represents a breach of the discourse. This self-policing is incessant, and transgressions of these intuited parameters are perceived as non-sensical.

Fourth and finally, it disciplines the dialogue about fiscal policy and debt management. Regardless of the delimited subjects, the discourse sets the "ways" in which specific topics should be discussed. Ideas that are up for discussion can only be addressed in certain ways. Not only must one focus upon government expenditures, for example, but the emphasis of the discussion must be on social programs, government inefficiency or government waste. It is beyond the range of acceptable discourse to talk about, for example, fiscal policy in terms of the federal government's recent operating surpluses. Similarly, although it is appropriate to talk about the cost of debt servicing, it is not appropriate to talk about the humanity of sustaining interest payments to wealthy individuals or to contrast their life styles with those of Canada's working poor.

In a more general sense, the debt discourse domesticates or colonizes understanding of deficits and the debt. Its ubiquity means that some discursive avenues are widely intuited as proper and appropriate while others are perceived as strange and off-the-wall. The presence of the discourse is highly visible in the media where the prevailing conversation regarding the debt scripts participants into bandying around comfortable affirmations, safe ideas and uncontentious recommendations. Any new information or declaration is mediated by the terminological universe of the discourse.

Thus, the discourse of fiscal crisis involves the routinization of discussion or the creation of uniformity in all talk about the debt and related fiscal matters. The same basic narrative on fiscal issues is played out again and again. At all times and in all mainstream venues an undifferentiated, predictable and inevitably prosaic story is reiterated ad nauseum. The debt story has only one ending.

The discourse of fiscal crisis, in summary, assigns seriousness, fixes truth, establishes the margins of debate, disciplines participants, domesticates understanding, confirms comprehension, mediates information and routinizes discussion. The debt discourse is widely internalized in a manner that respects speech boundaries and accords with social anticipation. In different terms, the congealed nature of the discourse is manifested in the widespread internalization of its conceptual menu on one side and the clear presence of competency standards and discursive uniformity on the other. It is a sealed and highly impermeable way of thinking, talking and acting about deficits and debt that has emerged over a relatively short time frame.

## The Resonance of the Discourse of Fiscal Crisis

The discourse of fiscal crisis has emerged very rapidly and been readily adopted by politicians and the public as a policy paradigm demanding neo-liberal solutions. The overhaul of the Canadian state—including, for example, privatization and the erosion of social assistance programs—is justified on the basis of impending fiscal doom. What has allowed the discourse of fiscal crisis to take such a firm hold and legitimize the ascendency of neo-liberal policies? What has allowed the evolution of Canadian finances to be represented as a crisis, a crisis that in turn catalyzes the neo-liberal agenda?

It is the primary contention of this book that the rationalizing power of the discourse of fiscal crisis is to be found in its resonance with an underlying *common sense*. The strength of the discourse arises from its consonance with a range of intersubjective ideas, narratives or themes embedded within popular consciousness (Taylor 1985). That is, the constellation of understandings that constitute the discourse are sheltered within an even wider tapestry of shared references and practices. Like all discourse, the discourse of fiscal crisis is rooted in a shared subjectivity. It rests upon a set of cultural intuitions that renders its content sensible. The sensibleness of the debt discourse, in short, is informed by a wide array of cultural referents.

This underlying or foundational intersubjectivity has three essential aspects. First, the discourse assumes history is a linear movement towards higher forms of civilization. The debt crisis is viewed as a dangerous historical aberation caused by profligacy. This sense of historical decay is underscored with metaphors of disease. Second, the structure and content of the debt discourse are consonant with tenets characteristic of a patriarchal consciousness. These include i) ideas of courage and sacrifice, ii) fears about the loss of control, iii) representations of fiscal policy and productive life that are abstract, iv) ideas of reasonableness and v) the voice of authority. Third, there are notions drawing on the culture of self-reliance, including the frequently drawn analogy between personal finances and state finances. These are the three concrete cultural referents that render the debt discourse sensible. In short, the debt issue has become discursively structured in terms that resonate easily within popular consciousness. The discourse "makes sense!"

The emphasis here is that the catalyzing power of the discourse is drawn from an intersubjective cradle. This has the profoundly important effect of making the heightened concern and prevailing representation of Canada's accumulating debt appear to be a matter of common sense. The discourse thus has the power of common awareness and sensibility. These elements of popular understanding make the hegemonic representation of the debt issue as a crisis sensible and, in turn, render neo-liberal solutions inherently meaningful or reasonable.

The debt discourse sounds comfortably familiar and commonsensical. It is helpful to locate this discussion in terms of the focus upon common sense understandings developed by Antonio Gramsci. I am not suggesting that the world view of the ruling class in Canadian society has simply achieved that status of common sense crucial to hegemonic rule. This notion certainly has considerable merit, and is reminiscent of Marx's reflections on class rule and intellectual life in *The German Ideology*: "The ideas of the ruling class are in every epoch the ruling ideas: i.e., the class which is the ruling material force of society is at the same time its ruling intellectual force. . . . For instance, in an age and in a country where royal power, aristocracy and bourgeoisie are contending for domination and where, there, domination is shared, the doctrine of the separation of powers proves to be the dominant idea and is expressed as an 'eternal law'" (Marx 1976).

Rather, the argument here draws attention to an intersubjective atmosphere that cradles and nurtures the ideas that support the implementation of a specific class agenda. Not all ideas will fly. Some ideas will get modified, some will sit awkwardly, still others will fade away. Indeed, this is consistent with Gramsci's discussion of the resistance of Europe to Fordist practices—a discussion which utilizes the language of "preliminary conditions," "Americanism," "particular environment" and "instinctive consciousness," all of which underscore the importance of a broader cultural fabric in the development of specific conjunctures, a fabric that is itself, of course, historically woven. The manner in which the discourse of fiscal crisis draws upon and reinvigorates this wider cultural canvas explains, perhaps more than anything else, its popular appeal despite the dramatic human toll associated with its neo-liberal policy implications.

Those who fail to talk about the debt in a manner consistent with the concepts and logic of the hegemonic discourse are shunted to the periphery and marginalized politically. Of course, nonconforming representations of the debt and deficit appear. To the extent that they provide dissenting reviews of the dominant debt discourse, they could be described appropriately as counter or critically discursive. An illustrative example of a critically discursive representation of the debt issue may be found in the work of the Canadian Centre for Policy Alternatives. The Centre's publications, such as *The Deficit Made Me Do It!: The Myths about Government Debt* (Chorney et al. 1992); *Bleeding the Patient: The Debt/Deficit Hoax Exposed* (Bienefeld n.d.); as well as the *Alternative Federal Budget 1995* (1995), co-produced with the Winnipeg-based CHO!CES: A Coalition for Social Justice, stand well outside the pale of the hegemonic debt discourse. Indeed, these ingenuous publications consistently attack every element of the prevailing discourse. In particular, they attack the "myth" of government overspending, draw attention to the role of interest rates and corporate tax breaks in the overall rise of the debt, attack the federal government's monetary policies, especially its interest rate policies, distinguish between public debt and private debt, question estimations of the overall size of the debt, attack large corporations and call for increased government spending in the economy.

Although counter-discursive representations appear in the media, they tend to receive very little overall attention, owing in part to their dissonant common sense ring. Thus, even when such understandings receive air-time, their location outside of the sphere of the hegemonic common sense discourse makes them easy targets. Moreover, these critical views tend not to be sustained to the degree that would be required to provoke a representational crisis.

## Crisis and Class Power

The discourse of fiscal crisis is linked profoundly to prevailing constellations of social power in Canadian society. In large measure, the neo-liberal agenda has become the new governing orthodoxy by virtue of its policy practices being legitimized by the dominant debt discourse. Debt issues provide the rationalizing wisdom for the "politics of scarcity" (Bakker 1995) practiced by the former Conservative government—and now a Liberal government —that is, the stress upon limited taxation and government cuts.

Policy prescriptions or full-blown agendas that fail to respect the exigencies of neo-liberal fiscal prudence necessarily are deemed to be irresponsible and unreasonable. Advocacy of increased government spending, a position that could easily flow from a variety of political standpoints, is eclipsed. All policy programs, especially those within political parties, are subordinated increasingly to the crucible of debt-cutting. In this sense, the discourse of fiscal crisis has promoted the narrowing of political considerations to issues of fiscal management and little else. The dynamics of class power become harder to see as they are reduced to a logical outcome. The narrow interests of capital appear as necessary, reasonable, universally benevolent alternatives.

Perhaps one of the clearest illustrations of the determinative power of the hegemonic discourse can be seen in the chorus of disapproval that greeted the 1991 budget of the Ontario New Democrats. The NDP budget responded to the deepening recession by increasing government spending and running a projected deficit that approached $10 billion. The NDP budget (a classic application of Keynesian counter-cyclical spending) confronted the growing wisdom surrounding the debt. As Thomas Walkom writes, "the ferocity of the reaction against the budget took the government by surprise. By 1991, it had become *accepted wisdom* in both business circles and the media that government debt was bad. However, the Rae government did not understand how deeply this neo-conservative [herein neo-liberal] orthodoxy had seeped into society. It did not understand that nerve—and lots of it—was required to run an economic policy directly counter to the *perceived wisdom* of television and radio talk shows" (1994: 103, emphasis added). In the end, the NDP, predictably, abandoned its Keynesian-style response to Ontario's recession and adopted policies that conformed to the predilections of large-scale capital.

The rationalizing nature combined with the common sense appeal of the discourse of fiscal crisis helps to explain the lack of sustained opposition to neo-liberal policies despite their startling human tolls. In the last two decades there has been a dramatic rise in poverty. Between 1973 and 1992 the number of families below the poverty line jumped by more than 40 per cent (Ross, Shillington and Lochhead 1994). For unattached individuals over the same period the poverty rate leapt by 79 per cent to 1.4 million. Among the provinces, Newfoundland, Quebec and Alberta were above the national average. The inclusion of Alberta is significant given the alacrity of the Klein government's attack on social assistance programs in the interest of debt reduction. For Canadian households of younger people, the rate of poverty jumped from 16.3 to 19.5 per cent between 1981 and 1991. The magnitude of poverty is considerably greater for single-parent families. Single-parent families with dependent children had a 54.2 per cent chance of living below poverty levels. For single mothers the picture was bleaker still. In 1981, the rate of poverty for mothers with children under 18 years reached 50.7 per cent. By 1991, the poverty rate had climbed to 58.1 per cent. The rate of poverty for single parents (typically mothers) with children of preschool age reached a dispiriting 69.2 per cent in 1991. Predictably, there was an accompanying rise in the incidence of poverty for children. According to the National Council of Welfare, the rate of poverty for children climbed from 14.9 per cent in 1980 to a staggering rate of 20.8 per cent in 1993 (National Council of Welfare 1995: 7–8).

Although measures of the scope and magnitude of poverty provide a rather crude indication of the changing nature of class relations, one striking conclusion of the Canadian Council on Social Development's assessment regarding the relationship between "market" wages and poverty in Canada must be stressed. For younger families in particular, it concludes that the worsening poverty is the result of "the inferior performance of market income." Its authors emphasize that an effective anti-poverty strategy should pay attention "to the number of jobs being created *and the wages and conditions attached to them*" (Ross et al. 1994: 119–20, emphasis added).

These observations bring us directly to a consideration of the effects of neo-liberal policies on the working class. The effects can be discussed in terms of worker vulnerability and downward pressure on wage rates. Most fundamentally, neo-liberal policies are designed to soften or condition labour markets. Indeed, some commentators describe the post-Fordist regime in terms of its greater flexibility with respect to labour (Harvey 1989). In part, this outcome has been achieved through the "freeing up" of new pools of labour, as evident in many regions of the South. It should be observed that a significant proportion of the newly released labour pool, up to 90 per cent in export processing zones, is made up of women who have been thrown off their small plots of land or are fleeing the shanty towns in search of ways to support their families. In the North, the conditioning of labour has been extended significantly by the basket of neo-liberal policies that includes deregulation (the resulting heightened competition and increased job insecurity both encourage a downward pressure on wages), privatization (where the new competitiveness and increased job insecurity also put downward pressure on wages), government downsizing (which increases the supply of unemployed labour and promotes lower wages), attacks upon trade unions (with the subsequent decline in the ability to withhold labour power), and the aggressive off-loading of tax burdens onto lower income stratas (which creates lower real wages).

These neo-liberal policies complement the dismantling of the welfare state, a strategy that greatly increases worker vulnerability by decreasing worker latitude and lowering job and wage expectations. At the same time, high levels of unemployment, or what has come to be called "structural unemployment," contribute to lower wage levels by increasing the pool of available labour, by fostering a greater sense of vulnerability and by lowering job expectations. There has been growth in part-time labour, a development that reduces the likelihood of benefits packages, pension schemes, and job security. The growth of contract work has had a similar impact. Likewise, strategies such as just-in-time production sometimes require workers to be available for short, intensive periods of work between dormant stretches. Again, the emergence of informal production schemes, especially in textiles, has transferred production costs directly to workers by, for example, forcing them to pay for their sewing machine, pay utilities and other carrying costs, and enlist their children's assistance. Finally, individual capitalists are able to use the threat of plant closures and relocation to extract concessions from local workers and revamp labour and wage standards across the economy. Programs such as the Free Trade Agreement and the North American Free Trade Agreement have accelerated these processes.

The toll of the neo-liberal agenda on the working class is evident. The very limited human relief or worker latitude created by social assistance packages is dissipating rapidly. Humiliating jobs that pay $5.00 an hour begin to look better than severely eroded social assistance benefits. The de facto tolerance of worker abuse grows as people feel increasingly vulnerable. A popular wisdom has emerged regarding the prized nature of a full-time job. As a disenchanted job retrainee from the Maritimes lamented on a regional CBC radio program, "everyone from around here knows, if you got one [a full-time job], hold onto it. Another one may not come along." Fighting for better working conditions can make one appear ungrateful. More and more people are taking a second job, establishing small businesses on the side, enlisting their children's labour in order to prop up family income, entering into double occupancy situations to reduce rental costs, off-loading family heirlooms, reducing grocery purchases, forgoing break-jobs on their car, and so forth in the face of mounting personal economic pressures. Unemployment and under-employment show signs of becoming the norm. The fear of lay-offs or dismissal is on the rise. Even the prospect of an altogether alienating but higher paying job attracts unprecedented attention, as was evident in the tens of thousand of people who lined up in the cold for a possible job with a General Motors assembly plant in Oshawa, Ontario, in January 1995.

This disciplining of labour is euphemistically referred to as making Canada more "globally competitive." The federal government has emphasized its leading role in wage restraint: "As a leading employer," observed Michael Wilson in his 1991 budget speech, "the government has a responsibility to ensure that public sector wage settlements do not add to inflationary pressures in the economy. . . . Wage settlements since 1987 have been lower than those concluded in the private sector and by provincial and municipal governments" (1991: 10). Moreover, as acknowledged in his budget address from a year earlier, the federal government has insured that real wages in the federal public sector have fallen: "Federal government wage increases have been below the inflation rate . . . since 1984" (1990: 10). Occasionally, the net effect of recent government policies upon labour is explicitly acknowledged. According to Linda McQuaig, Bank of Canada officials laud "structural unemployment" in the interests of controlling inflation (especially wage levels). As McQuaig writes of one Bank of Canada official that she interviewed, "in [his] view, the unemployment is needed to reinforce the message that workers must moderate their wage demands. It is the lash that will convince reluctant workers to accept lower wages" (McQuaig 1995: 151).

## A New Hegemony

There is an ongoing reconfiguration of class relations at work in Canadian society. The ascendency of neo-liberalism translates directly into the growing vulnerability of many segments of the working class and the intensified growth of a marginalized class. Neo-liberal policies are rolling back the hard-won gains of the working classes. It is an *undoing* as much as a *doing*.

There is evidence from polling data that the debt discourse has become a sense-giving and rationalizing force for neo-liberalism across all classes. As such, it has assisted in fostering a consensual basis for a reconstituted hegemony in Canadian society. The subaltern classes most vulnerable to the neo-liberal onslought lend considerable support to the neo-liberal policy program. The discourse of fiscal crisis draws affirmation and nods of consent from all corners of society. At least two findings from polling data supporting this argument warrant discussion. A critical reading of results is necessary in view of the leading nature of the questions of many polls. Often the questions force particular responses by linking undesirable answers (from the perspective of the polling agency) to widely unpopular policy options such as tax increases. For example, when polling on the degree of action that people feel is required on the deficit, an Angus Ried poll found that 74 per cent prefer either "steady, moderate reductions" (42 per cent), or that "the federal government should take whatever steps are necessary to significantly reduce the deficit" (32 per cent). However, the only other option had the federal government not worrying "too much about reducing the deficit" and instead "stimulating the economy." This last option is likely to be unappealing to the extent that stimulative action by the federal government is linked to tax hikes. It is much more prudent, therefore, to identify such polls as part of the ongoing process of hegemonic reconstitution itself, rather than as a barometer of such a process.

Still, some polls are informative regarding the creation of a consensual basis for the neo-liberal project. Poll findings suggest that there is a growing tendency to see Canada's fiscal situation as a crisis. A Decima Research poll from August 1994 (an off-budget and off-election period) without a context-setting lead-in question asked Canadians about their level of concern about the national debt and deficit. The poll asked individuals whether they believe the debt and deficit are "in a state of crisis," are "very serious problems, but not a crisis yet," or "are problems, but they are not that serious." Unfortunately, the poll did not allow for the identification of the debt and deficit as non-problems, and it could be argued that the options are imbued with notions of gravity and crisis, especially in the ordering of the options. Nonetheless, the poll did allow participants to identify the debt as a problem that is not that serious. Of those polled, 56 percent believe that Canada's fiscal situation is in a state of crisis. A further 37 per cent believe that the debt and deficit are "very serious problems." Only 6 per cent of those polled believe that the national debt and deficit are "not that serious." This finding is consistent with the idea that a sense of urgency has been constructed around the debt situation. Viewing fiscal matters with such gravity and foreboding is crucial to the creation of a rationalizing context for the neo-liberal agenda, especially if other policy programs are to be subordinated to deficit-cutting agendas.

A second finding, this time from a Gallop poll (1995), is consistent with the idea that a consensual basis for neo-liberal policies is emerging among

Canada's poorest groups. The finding of the poll supports the idea that significant numbers of all income groups, including lower-income individuals, believe that policy matters must be subordinated to deficit cutting. Participants were asked whether "the federal government should give top priority to reducing the deficit, even if it means maintaining a high level of employment" or "give top priority to reducing unemployment, even if it means maintaining a high deficit." The poll must be treated cautiously since it provided only two options, with each statement being linked to a (contentious) implication. Still, the poll does allow respondents stark options regarding government priorities. Among respondents making less than $40,000 per year, 42 per cent supported attacking the deficit. This figure fell to only 40 per cent for those earning less than $30,000 per year. Remarkably, almost one third of those polled (31 per cent) making less than $20,000 per year believed that the government should attack the deficit. These figures support the idea that a consensual basis is being established for neo-liberal policies among all classes (with the caveat that income stratification is only a crude indicator of class). That is, there is substantial support for an attack on the deficit in lieu of an attack on unemployment—a government out-of-the-economy position more generally—even among those groups most likely to be harmed by a such an approach, assuming that people on low incomes see government job creation policies as potentially elevating their annual incomes. Expressed more baldly, substantial components of those classes that can not afford fine leather belts support so-called belt-tightening measures by their government to avoid an impending fiscal "crisis."

## Conclusion

The discourse of fiscal crisis has served to justify and legitimize neo-liberal policies in Canada. As a supra-rationalizing framework it thereby has helped rupture a class compromise. Consequently, to the considerable extent that the discourse rationalizes and legitimizes policies that encroach upon subaltern classes and distinctly advantage capital, it can be said to be undergirding the reconstitution of class hegemony in Canadian society. There is a measurable human toll to this process. The scope and magnitude of poverty is clearly on the rise. Deregulation, privatization, government downsizing and streamlining, the attack upon labour unions, shifting tax ratios, and the dismantling of the welfare state combine with part-timing, outsourcing and flexible production schedules to heighten worker vulnerability and force real wages down. As the insecurity of everyday life rises, the expectation that the state will be there to help falls.

The catalyzing capacity of the discourse of fiscal crisis is due to its consonance with a backgrounded world-view that serves to render the discourse sensible and enliven it with meaningfulness. That is, the prevailing debt discourse is consonant with common sense ideas relating to personal finances and individual responsibility, to patriarchal consciousness and gendered life, and to the idea that history is advancing inexorably towards a greater good. Indeed, these shared cultural referents play a critical role in weaving and patterning the discourse. Therein lies the source of its strength and power.

CHAPTER THREE

# THE REPRESENTATION OF HISTORY AND THE DISCOURSE OF FISCAL CRISIS

The discourse of fiscal crisis is structured around a fundamental Western idea of history as a linear movement towards higher forms of civilization. This notion contrasts rather sharply with the understanding of human history as cyclical, that is, as a process where the past is inevitably repeated in the future ad infinitum. It also contrasts with linear views of history which emphasize the continual deterioration of civilization, an understanding sometimes expressed through ideas of "the fall" or through references to golden ages or eras of the past. The more prevalent view in Western thought is that human history will continually improve as we move through time. There is not a necessary telos in the unfolding of history, just the notion that the human condition will continually be enhanced and enriched. The challenge, therefore, for those who direct Western history is to insure that this inevitable historical line is not sidetracked or subverted by poor judgement, greed or selfishness.

The modernist idea of human progress is nested in this broader linear understanding of history. According to this view, the sustained application of human reason, especially as this is manifested through scientific thought, will contribute to the constant betterment of life. The lives of individuals will continually improve as the fruits of science release individuals from the trials and afflictions that characterize daily life. Societies will also be freed from the scourges of the past; through the careful application of reason and

41

science, they will overcome the calamities and plagues that have forever daunted humankind. In short, this idea of progress assumes the more rudimentary idea that historical evolution and change will result in the betterment of humankind.

A more contemporary version of this notion of history can be found in the writings that celebrate the end of the Cold War as the triumph of capitalism. These ideas, expressed recently in Francis Fukuyama's *The End of History and the Last Man*, differ from notions of continual improvement in that they have posited an endgame in the unfolding of history. Over the last century, capitalist apology has forecast the inevitable ascendency of individual freedom and liberal democracy. The collapse of the Soviet Union reinforced this faith. Capitalism becomes a phase in the normal historical betterment of humankind. This sanguine view can be summarized in Fukuyama's thesis that we may not have arrived at the end of history yet, but we most definitely can see it from where we stand.

The discourse of fiscal crisis is structured broadly in terms of the optimism regarding historical change and the view of evolution as continual betterment and improvement. According to the debt discourse, however, the trajectory of improvement has been subverted by profligacy and spendthrift policies. The path of history has been derailed by irresponsible governments pandering to the clamour of the public for the purpose of re-election, an understandable but dangerous human weakness. Massive indebtedness caused by human frailty and weakness constitutes the tragedy of the contemporary period. This notion of errant ways is underscored through the use of bodily metaphors of sickness and health. The apparent corruption of history is now portrayed as a debilitating disease. Only by ridding society of this terrible affliction of indebtedness can the course of history be righted.

In a society permeated by the idea that the future holds continual improvement, the presentation of the debt as destroying this trajectory is unsettling in a vague and undefined way. History, it seems, has been corrupted by the forces of prodigality. A concern for future generations understandably has arisen. Only the restoration of responsible fiscal policy will quell this unease. The progression of history can, and must, be returned to its proper course of frugality and responsibility to avoid undermining the lives of our children and grandchildren. The failure to do this will condemn future generations to a fiscal catastrophe, and thereby deprive them of the opportunity to enjoy the fruits of life that are deservingly theirs.

## The Road to Indebtedness
The discourse of fiscal crisis implicitly poses a straightforward question: "How did we reach a stage of massive indebtedness?" It also provides a

rather straightforward answer: "Profligacy and irresponsibility!" The debt discourse invariably identifies past government spending sprees as the direct cause of the debt morass. If governments had exercised greater levels of responsibility, if they had learned to be frugal and pennywise, then Canadians would not have become mired in debt. Moreover, the discourse adds that our debt situation would be even worse if governments had not financed their profligacy on the backs of tax-payers. This unfortunate combination of irresponsible spending and greedy taxation is invoked as the primary explanation for the debt.

The widespread understanding that the debt is due to government spending has very little merit. Program spending by federal and provincial governments was not high over the period that the debt accumulated. In fact, when the current ratio of government spending to overall GDP of 16 per cent is compared with levels of spending throughout much of the post-Second World War period it is apparent that government spending is now lower. Put simply, it has not increased as a proportion of the GDP, it has decreased. It is strange to characterize such a decrease as profligacy.

There is considerable evidence that the debt can be attributed to i) lost corporate tax revenues and ii) the costs of debt servicing. Both of these facts implicate governments, although not in sense that profligacy does. Declining revenues from corporate taxes have been attributed directly to the growth of the debt. A study by Statistics Canada in 1991 reveals that 50 per cent of the federal debt can be attributed directly to corporate tax breaks. A further 43 per cent is attributable to interest on the debt. Consequently, well under 10 per cent of the debt can be attributed to government spending (see McQuaig 1995: 52–63 for a discussion of the fierce opposition of the Department of Finance to this study by the state's statistical agency). In view of this, there has been growing criticism of the Bank of Canada's "tight" monetary policy and of its role in keeping interest rates high, a policy that increases debt-servicing costs. In light of this criticism, the C.D. Howe Institute has responded with spirited defences of the Bank of Canada's policy entitled "Don't Bet on the Bank: Monetary Policy and Canada's Growing Foreign Debt" (Robson 1993) and "Don't Break the Bank!: The Role of Monetary Policy in Deficit Reduction" (Laidlaw and Robson 1995).

## Twenty-five Years of Debt

A few examples will illustrate the prevailing history of the discourse of fiscal crisis. An example of the prevailing narrative of debt history can be found in the Canadian Broadcasting Corporation's special entitled *25 Years in Debt*. The program aired on Prime Time News in February 1995, just a few days before the release of Paul Martin's second budget. At the outset of the documentary, host Neil MacDonald draws attention to the sheer magnitude of the debt. While the audience is treated to a vivid graphic of burgeoning indebtedness MacDonald soberingly reminds them that "no one ever envisioned this." He then poses a very telling question: "How did we get into this *mess*? How did we ever get to the point where *overspending* by $30 billion constitutes some kind of financial *restraint*"(emphasis added). The answer to these pointed questions is quickly offered. "The history of the federal debt, of all these deficits," he retorts, "is a history of *procrastination*, of terribly *bad judgement*, of *cynical politics*, and of *drunken spending*" (emphasis added). The basic debt narrative is ensconced in the documentary at its outset. The listener is told in no uncertain terms that the condition of Canada's finances is grave, and an assortment of undesirable traits such as clouded thought and inebriation have brought Canadians to this point.

MacDonald then walks the viewer through a more detailed history of the debt. In 1970, the federal government had an operating surplus of $220 million. The public debt was "well within control" at a little less than $2 billion. Shortly thereafter John Turner, the Liberal finance minister, began to run up yearly deficits in the context of a series of global economic shocks. By the mid-1970s, the Liberal government had turned to "heavy spending" in order to stimulate the economy. MacDonald laments that "a lot of that spending didn't work," and equates Liberal spending with expanding government: "Big government exploded during the 1970s. Ottawa increased its reach into the lives of individual Canadians and of businesses." Moreover, the viewer is told that the Liberal government failed to heed the warning of experts about "the dangers of such overspending." The documentary then shifts to a clip of Liberal Finance Minister Donald MacDonald, a clip meant to suggest that there was a preoccupation with issues of the day and an indifference to the effect of government spending upon future generations of Canadians. By the close of the 1970s, the federal government debt had "lifted off" to $64 billion. A sense of acceleration of indebtedness is also cultivated by emphasizing the relative size of yearly deficits: "That year [1979], the government ran a deficit of 13 billion dollars, nearly six times the size of the deficit *only* four years earlier" (emphasis added).

"All the while," the narrator reminds the viewer, "the Conservatives watched righteously from opposition, anxious to get into power and put an end to this *tomorrow-be-damned spending*" (emphasis added). With the election of the Conservatives in 1979, an opportunity to reverse the over-spending trend was lost. In fact, MacDonald interprets the subsequent defeat of the minority Tory government in terms of its refusal to run up high deficits. In the first Tory budget John Crosbie "threw himself on the sword of doing the right thing." His efforts to "trim spending" and raise gasoline taxes (all in the spirit of balancing the budget) the viewer is told, prompted the defeat of the minority government. "In the election that followed,"

MacDonald tells the viewer, "it became exceedingly clear that voters were not interested in *restraint*, even the *mild kind of restraint* being proposed by John Crosbie" (emphasis added). At this point an interview portion is inserted whereby Crosbie is asked "So you paid the price for trying to do the right thing?" He responds that he was indeed "'trying to do the right thing. But we—but we went about trying to do it stupidly.'"

To underscore the point that the wrong thing was done throughout the 1980s, Pierre Trudeau's well-known quip "'Well, welcome to the 1980s'" is inserted in a timely fashion. "And, welcome back to spending. . . ." MacDonald reminds the viewer, "Allan MacEachen's 1980 budget talked little of the deficit, but of quote—major new expenditures in energy, economic development, industrial adjustment and manpower training—unquote." Again, to emphasize the idea of indifferent profligacy, MacDonald inserts a quote of then Finance Minister Marc Lalonde: "'The temporary increase in the deficit—But what can you do? You know, this is life.'" MacDonald then rhetorically asked the audience "So what did he do?" In a tone of exasperation and bewilderment he responds to his own question by emphasizing that Lalonde, working on the assumption that oil revenues would rise, "spent billions on nearly a hundred federal projects, and a whole series of federal projects, and a whole series of taxes." He then returns to his ethical leitmotif: "In early 1984, . . . even as he spent, Lalonde knew he was not doing the right thing." When the second Trudeau era came to an end, the federal debt "had nearly doubled . . . in just one term of government."

With the arrival of the Conservative government in 1984 Brian Mulroney, MacDonald observes, was promising jobs and preaching financial restraint. The viewer is told that the Tory government was more sensitive to fiscal matters. To this end Michael Wilson, the new Conservative minister of finance, tried to cut back old age pensions. He faced stiff opposition from senior citizens who forced the Tory administration to back off. The documentary then shifts back to Crosbie: "I think that if there had been any chance that we were going to do anything in a major way with social programs, that's where it got stopped right there, by this [pension] decision."

At this point the culprit behind the expanding federal debt is identified as the spending on government programs. The debt-sensitive Tories, according to MacDonald, took to raising taxes instead: "instead of cutting spending significantly, the Tories proceeded to raise taxes. Every year seemed to bring new grabs—personal tax hikes, business tax hikes, surtaxes on personal taxes. At the same time, the Tories closed exemptions and reduced deductions." The Tories had an opportunity to attack the debt, MacDonald concludes, but missed it: "all the while, the debt just sat there, growing to monstrous proportions. Most experts now agree there was never a better time to slash spending and attack the debt than during the rich booming 1980s. The Tories had that opportunity and did not do it." A clip of Marc Lalonde underscores the basic idea of a lost opportunity: "'They didn't have the guts to do it . . . . And I'm sorry about that. I think that was a missed opportunity, and no surprise, you know, that in the meantime, the debt more than doubled, and we are where we're at today.'"

As the documentary winds down, MacDonald concludes that political considerations have forced governments into over-spending. "Despite speeches by people like Brian Mulroney about leaders having to make the tough choices," he claims, "they didn't." There is a rudimentary structural defect in electoral democracies that encourages overspending: "Modern governments go only as far as their own polling tells them they can go. In other words, the Canadian public insisted on all of that *colossal overspending*" (emphasis added). The debt, in short, is a product of political pandering of the worst sort. The documentary, aired just days before the budget, concludes by stressing that the lesson has yet to be learned: "And Finance Minister Paul Martin is poised to add to it again."

The CBC documentary is not unique, exceptional or idiosyncratic. An article in the *Whitehorse Star* of April 1995 entitled "Expert traces history of national debt" reveals a similar narrative structure. As with the CBC documentary, it begins by emphasizing the gravity of the debt: "You have politicians of all stripes at the federal and at provincial levels continually going around and telling you, 'Don't worry, everything is going to be okay. We've got this situation very much under control. . . .' We shouldn't be lulled into complacency about this because we're paying for this with more taxes, and young people will be paying for it for the rest of their lives."

With the seriousness of the issue established, the article then offers an account of the debt that focuses directly on government spending: "In the mid-1960s, the Government of Canada made a fundamental decision to change the way it was going to finance the future. . . . The federal government told the provinces that if they wanted to share in national standards, it would match each provincial dollar invested." The reader then learns that the provinces, predictably, jumped at this offer, although the "federal government never built in an automatic mechanism for adjustment to reduce expenditures in case too much was being spent." With this information the anticipated link between indebtedness and government spending has been forged. "With no checks on expenditures," the article continues, "more was spent and the deficit grew." The election of the Tories did nothing to stem the debt tide: "When the Conservatives were elected in the early '80s, they realized something had gone terribly wrong . . . but essentially did absolutely nothing about the problem the Liberals got them into during the '70s." The article then concludes by necessarily linking the debt to government cutbacks: "Now we're faced with draconian budget slashing measures."

Both pieces are illustrative of a few basic elements of the prevailing debt narrative. First, there is the notion of run-away government spending as the key cause of Canada's continuing fiscal woes. For example, a *Globe and Mail* editorial from 27 November 1993, entitled "Alberta shows the way," lauds the deficit reduction efforts of the Klein government in Alberta and chastises the Ontario government for failing to understand the implications of "allowing the debt snowball to get rolling" (D6) shortly after the latter province's credit rating had been down-graded. A *Globe and Mail* editorial from 6 January 1995, entitled "The folly of raising taxes," puts the matter even more bluntly: "The government does not have a shortage of revenue; it has a surfeit of spending" (A18).

A common metaphor that surfaces to underscore the idea of run-away government spending is that of digging holes. An exemplary C.D. Howe Institute commentary entitled "Digging Holes and Hitting Walls" (Robson 1994) is structured around this metaphor. The analysis emphasizes that by refusing to lower government spending the government is effectively "digging holes." It suggests that a credit crisis for Canada might be beneficial if such a crisis were to "jolt the shovels out of our hands." With some predictability, it calls upon federal and provincial governments to cut their deficits in "an order of magnitude greater than those seen to date." In 1990, the federal government introduced an Expenditure Control Plan that froze or reduced government spending for a two year period. According to the minister of finance, the program was designed to "restrain" the growth in government program spending, with the clear implication that theretofore government spending had an *unrestrained* character about it. In short, the commonly expressed notion of "reining in" government spending or getting the "deficit under control" implicitly underscores the idea that fiscal matters are now out of control.

This notion of unrestrained government spending is complemented by the idea of government mismanagement. To elaborate initially on the idea of ability, government profligacy is associated directly with poor managerial skills. In a CBC *Prime Time News* segment that addressed the NDP budget on 23 April 1993 (with the Ontario budget being introduced by Peter Mansbridge as "the mother of all deficits"), Catherine Swift, a chief economist for the Canadian Federation of Independent Business, clearly established the link between debt and government mismanagement: "I guess with groups like ours who have been telling of this impending financial crisis on the part of the Ontario government for years, it's a bit tough to have a whole lot of sympathy at this point that they [the government] finally reap the harvest of their own financial mismanagement." A *Globe and Mail* editorial from 21 December 1994, entitled "Mr. Rae on Windmills," rather bluntly states that the Ontario government is being called to account for its finances by Bay Street and the general public because of the Rae government's "monumental mishandling of the public's money" (A22).

It must be stressed that the partisan nature of this commentary is quite distinct from the ideas used to express partisanship. Less overtly partisan assessments are common. In an address to the House of Commons Standing Committee on Finance, for example, Tom D'Aquino, president of the Business Council on National Issues, drew attention to fifteen years of "fiscal mismanagement" rooted in "a failure of political leadership" (1994: 5), which he sees as lying at the heart of Canada's debt crisis.

Along with being mismanaged, governments are considered to be irresponsible or undisciplined. The federal finance minister, Paul Martin, in his 1995 budget speech, bluntly identified previous periods of government carelessness as the reason for his harsh measures: "We would not have to reduce spending as much as we do if that spending was under better control in the first place" (1995: 15). A year earlier, Martin had been even more direct in his assessment of the problem: "It is time to restore fiscal responsibility to the public finances of Canada" (1994: 13). A revealing *Globe and Mail* editorial from 8 March 1993 entitled "Hang together, or hang separately" chides the spending habits of the provincial governments. The editorial aggressively attacks the notion of baseline budgeting (that is, assessing and projecting fiscal policy on the basis of previous budgets) as fundamentally undisciplined:

> Until now, the standard of parsimony was this: Party A, after running up double-digit spending increases for years on end, is voted out of office. Party B takes power with a pledge to rein in spending. This, it turns out, means taking the grotesquely swollen budget left them by their profligate predecessors, and increasing it—but at a slower rate. With that definition of fiscal discipline, it is not surprising that Canada should have rung up the largest public debt, per capita, in the world. (A12)

Edward Newall, CEO of NOVA Corporation and chair of the BCNI, expressed the matter even more baldly: "We are now well into a second decade of a style of fiscal management that borders on irresponsibility" (Newall 1994: 5).

In the context of a firmly entrenched debt discourse, however, not all governments appear equally indifferent to the good of Canadians. An earlier *Globe and Mail* editorial from 27 February 1991 cautiously praises the federal finance minister, Michael Wilson, for his "proper emphasis on the discipline Canada needs" (A14). It adds: "The discipline will be found, either in our own policy or in the far more brutal workings of global financial markets." Another *Globe and Mail* editorial from 2 August 1994 extolls the propriety of New Zealand's Fiscal Responsibility Act, an act that it glowingly describes as a "self-tailored strait jacket." The editorial concludes by pointing out that Canada has avoided catastrophe only because of its economic breadth and not because its leaders have acted responsibly: "Unlike little New Zealand, we have never had a crisis. Pity" (A16).

The outcome of all this government mismanagement and profligacy is established unequivocally by the discourse of fiscal crisis. First of all, years of over-spending have created inefficient, unwieldy governments. In February 1990, in the context of emphasizing his reduction in government expenditures, Michael Wilson proudly announced that "waste is being eliminated. Productivity has been improved; it will be further improved by measures in this budget. We will continue to seek out ways to eliminate waste and inefficiency in the months and years ahead." John Richards, a contributor to C.D. Howe publications from Simon Fraser University, offered an assessment of the Axworthy review of the Canadian social programs on CBC's *Prime Time News* in 4 February 1994 that was typical of the discourse: "Many of these programmes are inefficient and Mr. Axworthy is to be praised for starting this major Canadian national dialogue and how do we render them more efficient." A *Globe and Mail* editorial from the same month rather baldly identifies unrestrained government spending with ballooning governments: "Ask yourself, in 1975, the last year the books were balanced, was there any noticeable shortage of government?" (14 February 1994: A12).

## The Debt Discourse and Bodily Health

In summary, according to the debt discourse the last two decades comprise an era of false plenty and spendthriftiness that has brought Canadians to the verge of disaster. It was an era in which Canadians lived beyond their means, partaking in a lavish life of indulgence. At this point in the discourse, the sense of historical change or evolution of Canadian society plugs directly into contemporary notions concerning illness and wellness of the body. Government profligacy and decay is presented as having moved us away from a condition of fiscal health into an era of actual or close-at-hand fiscal sickness. As Don Mazankowski claims in his summary of the last Tory budget in 1993: "That is what this budget is all about. It charts a responsible, achievable course to increase the job-creating potential of our economy and to secure the financial health of government" (1993: 17). A *Globe and Mail* editorial from 5 February 1992 stresses that the cure to poor fiscal health must employ the appropriate antidote: "It makes little sense to advise the government to spend its way out of the recession [the Keynesian approach is clearly the wrong prescription]. This downturn is very different from the plunge we experienced in the Great Depression. And that means different methods have to be used to cure the economic diseases that afflict us. You do not mend a broken leg by performing triple-bypass heart surgery; you do not solve a problem of over-indebtedness by encouraging further indebtedness" (A12).

One of the clearest examples of the analogy to bodily health appears in publications of the Fraser Institute in Vancouver. The Fraser Institute derivatively draws upon the work of the World Bank regarding the nature and scope of a country's indebtedness. Using two measurements in particular, the ratio of debt servicing costs to gross national product and the ratio of debt servicing costs to exports, the World Bank has produced a list of "severely indebted countries." Using the acronym SIC, the World Bank has compiled a SIC-list, that is, a listing of countries that are considered to be severely indebted. The intimation in the acronym is straightforward: SIC→sick. Inspired by the work of the World Bank, the Fraser Institute has developed its own SIC-list, which also addresses the federal and provincial governments in Canada. The results of the Fraser's analysis are published as a special issue of the *Fraser Forum: Inside Canada's Government Debt Problem and the Way Out* (Richardson 1994).

The federal government and all of the provincial governments make the SIC-list. According to the study, the most severely indebted province is Newfoundland and the least indebted (but still heavily indebted) province is Alberta. Only the Northwest Territories and the Yukon miss the list, appearing as MICs or "moderately indebted countries." Indeed, nine Canadian provinces and the federal government all appear among the SIC(est) fifty states in the world according to the Fraser Institute. Alberta, the site of the so-called Klein revolution, appears fifty-first on the Fraser Institute's SIC list. An effective graphic of the world colours in all of the severely indebted countries with black, which has the effect of blackening all of Canada along with most of the countries in Africa and South America, leaving Europe and the United States white. With many Canadian provinces appearing to be SIC(er) than countries such as Burundi, Rwanda, Ethiopia and Myanmar, the Fraser's conclusion is not at all surprising: "Canada has joined the Third World in terms of the magnitude and severity of its total all-government debt problem. All of the conditions for a financial crisis of major proportions are now in place" (48). The Fraser Institute wittingly appeals to the unselfconscious racism of its supporters, but at times its racist notions of superiority are expressed more directly. "In other words," concluded Peter C. Newman after reviewing Canada's debt servicing costs in *Maclean's* in 8 May 1989, "Canada is not only bankrupt, we rank right up there with the world's worst debtor countries—a sort of Zaïre with polar bears" (48).

On other occasions the debt situation is likened to insanity and addiction. A *Globe and Mail* editorial from 16 January 1995 (one month before the release of the second Liberal budget in Canada) titled "Restraint American-style" provides a typical example of the links made to mental health. In its discussion of American restraint legislation, including the Gramm-Rudman-Hollings Act and the 1990 Budget Enforcement Act, measures adopted by the United States Congress in order to limit the growth of the American debt, the editorial states that the American deficit is expected to decline to 3.5 per cent of its gross domestic product in 1995 (the editorial immediately adds that the Canadian deficit is expected to be 5.4 per cent). However, according to the editorial, the discretionary limits on American spending will run out in 1998, and legislators there are searching for new ways to impose limits. The language used to underscore the gravity of this situation is both inflammatory and discriminatory: "What to do? Like the psychopath who shouts 'Stop me before I kill again,' the new Republican-led Congress wants to bind its own hands with a balanced-budget amendment to the U.S. Constitution" (A12). Claims that government fiscal policy is "mad" or "insane" are common. In a speech in Ottawa in the late 1980s Tom d'Aquino of the BNCI called for "a return to fiscal sanity, knowing full well that sound public finances will engender the most precious ingredient of economic success—confidence and trust" (1989). Another *Globe and Mail* editorial from 13 February 1995 bemoans the prospect of tax increases and draws an analogy to alcoholism: "You do not help a man with a drinking problem by refilling his glass" (A12).

The recent history of fiscal policy is represented in terms that accord directly with modern intuitions about the body as something that can be managed—usually through physical regimentation and diet—to maintain health. The analogical implication is that the Canadian state has become infirm as a result of neglect and carelessness (not unlike failing to exercise and eating poorly). A sampling of the language is revealing. We live in an era of "big government" that has a "monstrous appetite for borrowing." The strategy is to exercise discipline, to take "bitter pills" with a view to restoring fiscal health. The healthy goal in this era is to "trim fat" from the public service, to create a "smaller government" with better social reflexes. Like a terminally ill patient receiving palliative care, "Canada's fiscal situation will continue to degenerate over the next couple of years" (Robson 1994: 23). In 1991 the Tory government proudly announced that it had "waged a long, uphill battle" in its efforts to restore fiscal health to Canada. "Our aim is not fiscal remission," Paul Martin told his luncheon guests at the Canadian Society of New York in early March 1995, "it's full fiscal health" (*The Toronto Star*, 4 March 1995). As Canada's fiscal situation worsens in the eyes of some, there are increasing calls for "radical surgery."

History is off its track. The metaphor of disease carries an unambiguous message with it. This aspect of the discourse is very powerful. The prevailing representation of Canada's fiscal condition rests upon something very elementary, almost innate. In other words, the discourse is not constructed around socially obscure understandings but rather those that are shared widely, if not universally.

## Future Generations

Along with the cultivation of the notion that history is off-course, there is a consequent forward-looking concern in the discourse of fiscal crisis. It holds that past excess, waste and carelessness has been tantamount to mortgaging the future of children. If careless government spending is continued unabated, future generations of Canadians will bear the burden. To avoid this, responsible fiscal policy must be initiated. Things can improve, but only if we work to establish these conditions through sensible spending. The maintenance of acceptable standards of living for future generations is contingent upon bringing government spending under control in the present.

Edward Newall, chair of the BCNI, draws direct links between the debt and future generations in his autumn 1994 speech circulated with the title *Canada's Future: Facing Up to Our Responsibilities*. Newall begins with a straightforward statement of fact regarding the debt: "When my father retired in 1964, our national debt was about $17 billion dollars. Given our population at the time, that represented about $900 dollars per Canadian. Of course, we had to pay interest on that debt. The cost of that interest, spread among all Canadians, was less than $40 dollars per person per year." He then cites a per capita income in Canada in 1964 of $1,750, and thus the interest payments on the debt, he calculates, were equal to about 2 per cent of personal disposable income. Newall then stresses: "So, when my father retired and his generation passed the torch to us, our national debt was very low, and provincial debt was negligible." To this point in his talk Newall stresses the manageability of the debt. However, the burdens of Canada's indebtedness increased quickly thereafter. "When my daughter presented us with our first grandchild in 1982," Newall continues, "on drawing his first breath, his share of the combined federal and provincial debt was about $6,400 dollars. Remember that my father's generation owed less than $1,000 dollars per person. In just 18 years, total government debt had grown more than six times over." The rapid increase in government debt, we are told, has brought us to a situation that is alarming according to Newall: "Today, at the ripe old age of twelve, my grandson's share of the total government debt has grown faster than he has. The debt has skyrocketed to over $26,000 per person. . . . Today, the interest of the debt eats up more than 12 per cent of disposable income." Newall concludes by stressing that the threat that this poses for future generations is profound: "At the turn of the century . . . my grandson's generation will be leaving high school. By then, the per capita debt will likely be more than $30,000. . . . My grandson will lose 13 per cent of this disposable income in perpetuity to pay interest on government debt—debt that was generated because my generation has been living beyond its means." Newall's account leads to an obvious conclusion: "My generation's mismanagement of the economy has created a burden for generations to come."

Other examples of the forward-looking aspect of the discourse abound. Federal Finance Minister Paul Martin's inaugural budget provided the following rationale for its fiscal direction: "During our pre-budget conferences, the point was made that the debt and the deficit burden pose much more than an economic challenge. This is a moral issue too. What right do we have to steal opportunity away from our children, to demand that they solve problems that we are too timid to face?" Martin immediately added anecdotally, "at one conference, a participant put it this way, '. . . if you have to cut . . . begin with me, because I refuse to be part of the system that is robbing the wealth out of the mouths of my children, our children'" (1994: 13). Drawing upon similar themes, a highly partisan *Globe and Mail* editorial from 6 May 1994 calumniates the fiscal policy of the Ontario NDP and accuses them of having "contempt for future generations who will have to pay for this four-year fiscal frenzy" (A26). "Let's not shamelessly place on the shoulders of our children and grandchildren," admonished Tom d'Aquino of the BCNI, in an address to the Kiwanis Clubs of Ottawa in the late 1980s, "the burden of our excesses" (23 February 1989: 11).

My concern does not lie with the intellectual veracity of the concerns voiced with respect to the future of our children. There are serious problems in this respect, especially with an approach that measures the quality of life in terms of levels of indebtedness rather than growing worker alienation, rising poverty, continuing abuse of women, and so forth. Our concern, rather, lies with the recognition that this aspect of the discourse of fiscal crisis is consonant with a fundamental understanding that the future will continue to get better. An overwhelming sense is fostered that this better future, however, is jeopardized by contemporary carelessness, profligacy and indifference. There is evidence that these ideas have extended to future generations themselves. A CBC *Prime Time News* segment from 26 April 1993 finds similar concerns expressed by high school students. "It's sickening," according to one student, "because . . . the government got us into it, didn't they? And . . . here we are, the people having to pay taxes to pay off the debt. We can't do anything about it now." As this point, a second student adds: "It's frustrating because we really didn't get Canada into this position in the first place, so we don't feel that in the long term we should have to get it out."

There is an added element to this aspect of the debt discourse. By drawing attention to concerns for future generations the discourse wraps itself up with concerns shared by parents about their position as parents. In this sense, the discourse is interpolated into widely shared sentiments regarding parenthood (sentiments that have been sharpened undoubtedly by the rapidity of change and heightened sense of personal vulnerability endemic to later capitalism). All parents want their children to "have an easier time of it." The discourse of fiscal crisis plays into these very understandable concerns.

## Conclusion

A critical reason for the resonance of the discourse of fiscal crisis in contemporary political life surrounds its consonance with notions of insuperable historical progress. In essence, the trajectory of history is characterized by constant movement towards higher forms of human civilization. This understanding has been intensified with the collapse of the Soviet Union and the end of the Cold War. In the context of this very rudimentary conviction that things will tend to move from bad to good, the discourse of fiscal crisis posits a recent history characterized by profligacy and indifference. These erring ways of governments have brought us to a period of crisis. Only by shedding antiquated ideological blinders and atavistic political reflexes, that is, only by accepting the lessons of the end of the Cold War, can we advance out of the present fiscal morass.

The representation of the present era as a crisis is intertwined with contemporary notions of bodily health and well-being. Once again, an intersubjective tapestry colours and shapes the discourse of fiscal crisis, a canvas of consciousness that helps to account for the resonances of the discourse within Canadian society. That is, widely intuited understandings of healthiness and sickness, of sanity and insanity, of the body as something that can be managed from a state of illness to a state of well-being and can be rendered more efficient through regimentation and care, all enter into the prevailing representation of the current fiscal situation. Consequently, the representation of Canada as fiscally feeble owing alternatively to insanity or slothful indulgence makes sense. As such, through more careful management of government finances and general moderation, the state can enter a period of fiscal convalescence and, hopefully, become healthy again.

CHAPTER FOUR

# GENDERED LIFE AND THE DISCOURSE OF FISCAL CRISIS

The discourse of fiscal crisis is constituted partially through gendered understandings characteristic of patriarchal culture. The very understandings and practices that lie at the heart of patriarchal society help to structure the debt discourse and imbue it with sensibility and meaningfulness. The elementary dualisms of patriarchal consciousness—man/woman or masculine/feminine or manliness/womanliness—inform and contour various elements of the debt discourse. More specifically, many of the rudimentary aspects of the discourse accord (implicitly and explicitly) with the masculine dimension of patriarchal culture and repudiate its feminine dimension, an accordance that gives it credibility and authority from the perspective of popular Canadian culture. The consonance of the discourse of fiscal crisis with patriarchal consciousness gives it a profound common sense quality.

I will elaborate upon the terms and ideas employed here, beginning with the notion that the debt discourse rests upon patriarchal culture. This is a historically constructed culture framed in terms of a series of dualistic or dichotomous understandings of manliness and womanliness, masculine and feminine, man and woman. Man and woman, therefore, are understood as social creations. These essentially cultural poles tend to correspond to the biological categories of male and female. In other words, a panoply of cultural oppositions around masculinity and femininity have emerged out of the species opposition of male and female.

The dualistic understanding of manliness and womanliness tends to inform most practices and experiences of life. The entire social world invariably is interpreted and structured in terms of these cultural axes. The notions of man and woman simultaneously inflect social practices and form an interpretative filter for them. The cultural understandings of man and woman are one of the most fundamental intersubjective cradles of contemporary life. The term gender is normally applied to these socially constructed categories of man and woman while the concept of sex is reserved for biological differences, and our interest here is in how the former function as a shared interpretative framework that must be respected by public speech and that give such speech meaning and authority.

A series of simple dichotomies corresponding to human qualities or traits were assigned over time in the West and elsewhere to the ideas of man and woman. Man became associated with mind, woman with body; man with reason, woman with emotion; man with thought, woman with intuition; masculinity with the public sphere, femininity with the private sphere; the masculine with the political, the feminine with the personal, and so on. Different spheres of human practices are in turn constructed in terms of these elaborated cultural categories of man and woman. In the area of work, for example, manly work is perceived as productive, skilled, formal, paid, breadwinning and worthy of a wage remuneration while woman's work is seen as reproductive, unskilled, informal, unpaid, homemaking and unworthy of remuneration (except for pin money). A complex and unrelenting set of understandings regarding men and women, what they do and what they should do became relatively fixed over a shorter (e.g., the era of late capitalism) period of social history. These basic understandings or narratives of gender constitute archetypical intersubjectivities for other cultural and practical arenas of life. Basic gender archetypes, for example, routinely are used even to structure popular media forms such as television situation-comedy plot lines.

Another crucial point must be made at this juncture. The elaborate cultural constructions of masculinity and femininity are not assigned equal social respect, value or human worthiness. Gender constructs are weighted heavily in favour of the masculine sphere. Invariably, those human qualities or practices perceived as most valuable or worthy of emulation are assigned to the masculine side of life, while those human qualities deemed to be less valuable or less useful are ascribed to the feminine. Patriarchal culture, in other words, involves the privileging of those characteristics perceived to be masculine. This privileging is essentially a masculinist interpretation of human qualities. In many respects, those qualities perceived as feminine constitute a negation of masculinity. For example, in a world where reason and contemplation are prized greatly, the feminine is perceived as unreasonable (emotional) and uncontemplative (intuitive). This unrelenting repudiation of things feminine can be described as a basic misogynistic reflex embedded in the heart of Western patriarchy. Womanliness has evolved to be a contemptible condition. The implied presence of feminine characteristics in any sphere of life undermines its status. This reaches its logical extreme in the idea that woman corrupts and destroys—encapsulated in the myth that Pandora was sent as a punishment to Prometheus. This is a foundational narrative of gender in Western culture.

A couple of additional aspects of patriarchal culture must be added to this overview. First, as with the entire intersubjective tapestry of modern life, the culture of gender is learned by all people according to strict rules of acculturation. On the whole, males are expected to interiorize masculine scripts and females are expected to interiorize feminine scripts. Males and females are normally positioned by gendered culture in terms of expectations and evaluations. Males, for example, are expected to act manly and the failure to do so will invite harsh assessments. Of course, males and females never perfectly internalize these masculine and feminine scripts. As finished cultural artifacts men and woman evince all sorts of inconsistencies, blemishes, contradictions and interruptions when measured against the writs of masculinity and femininity. Nonetheless, a very strict process of social sanctioning and disciplining tends to ensure that most males come to be masculine and females largely come to be feminine.

Finally, the critical effect or outcome of gendered culture is the oppression of women. The privileging of masculinity, combined with racism and classism, places men in a position of power, both in terms of their relative capacity to pursue goals and, equally importantly, directly over women. By comparison with a man, a woman's daily life tends to typically involve greater hardship, toil and vulnerability. Many opportunities afforded to men are closed off to women. A woman's ability to pursue goals is frustrated frequently by all manner of blockages, hazards or disciplinary and dissuasive epithets. Women typically can achieve recognition and power more easily by adopting masculine characteristics and suppressing those understood as feminine, with Margaret Thatcher being a widely identified recent example.

The skewed relations of power between men and women within patriarchal culture animates feminist politics in a fundamental sense. Nonetheless, it is helpful to observe that masculine and feminine constructs inhibit the rounded human growth of both males and females by necessitating the atrophy of some human qualities and demanding the over-development of others. In other words, gender constructs are imprisoning. They are the equivalent of humanity suppressants for both males and females, notwithstanding their egregious effects on the latter.

Patriarchal consciousness, in short, comprises the gendered understandings and practices that infuse all walks of men's and women's daily condition. It forms a crucial common sense backdrop for our everyday world. The discourse of fiscal crisis is not aloof to this aspect of contemporary life. The complex of cultural codes and symbols that constitute patriarchy enter into the debt discourse at a number of different points. These gendered intersections of the debt discourse give it social credibility and a definitive ring of common sense.

More specifically, the debt discourse contains numerous elements that relate most clearly to the masculine side of life, and consequently resonate with intuitive sensibility and authority across Canadian society. The clearest example of this relationship is the language of courage and resolve. Acknowledging the gravity of the debt condition, indeed, recognizing that the debt is a "crisis," requires courage. Fiscal management through the crisis is not for the faint of heart. It requires the courage to act. It demands sacrifice. The realm of debt management requires fortitude and a resolute steadfastness against the forces of prodigality. Second, there is a very strong motif of maintaining control, particularly over fiscal affairs. The federal debt and government spending are seen as being out of control, a condition that is self-evidently alarming. There is the concern that government control of state programs—expressed as the sovereignty of Canada—might fall to foreign money lenders or the International Monetary Fund unless fiscal thriftiness is restored. Third, the discourse of fiscal crisis is infused with the tendency to speak about the debt and the economy in purely abstract terms. The discourse is replete with measurements and indicators that reflect very little of the lived experiences of people. This use of abstraction helps assign a sort of deductive truth to assertions that underline the basic debt narrative. This aspect of the discourse feeds into the fourth gendered dimension, that is, the terms of the prevailing debt discourse are presented as straightforward and reasonable. Plans for deficit reduction simply are wise plans. Within the prevailing discursive atmosphere, any claims that the debt is not a problem become unreasonable claims. Anyone who endorses policies that do not respect the logic of deficit reduction appears unwise. Fifth, the debt discourse is voiced with absolute authority. The discourse of fiscal crisis is father speaking. Debt realities are not subjects for debate; they are truths best conveyed through paternal postures, serious demeanours, well-cut apparel and stern faces. The declarations of incontrovertible truths, to employ a cliché, uttered by those who know best, position the public as children.

The presence of these qualities within the *discourse of fiscal crisis* is critical to its wider credibility and reception. As a consequence of these gendered intersections, practices that are highly politicized, that maintain power and privilege and that contribute to greater human hardship are mystified and legitimized. In short, the basic accordance of the debt discourse with manliness and the explicit and implicit repudiation of feminine qualities are integral to its wider reception. A debt discourse permeated with qualities perceived as feminine would lose credibility and authority. Indeed, it would be confusing and non-sensical to the general public.

Below is an expansion of each of these intersections between the discourse of fiscal crisis and patriarchal consciousness.

## The Debt-fighters

One salient aspect of gender is the association of manliness with bravery, courage and sacrifice. The notions of bravery, courage and sacrifice have often been identified with soldiering, perhaps the quintessential male undertaking. Closely related characteristics such as firmness and resolve are also part of the masculine framework. The discourse of fiscal crisis is replete with ideas of courage, bravery and sacrifice. Indeed, these three notions form nodal points for a representation of the hegemonic debt discourse. In brief, politicians must have the courage to acknowledge the gravity of the debt. They must be brave enough to take firms steps so that the crisis can be resolved. Political leaders must call upon all members of society to make sacrifices in view of Canada's looming fiscal crisis. These aspects are readily observable in the frequent assertions that Canadians are up against a formidable foe and that tough times are inevitable. This setting of the fiscal battlefield, in a sense, is central to all budget speeches. As Don Mazankowski soberingly reminded Canadians in his 1992 budget address: "Times are difficult. There are serious economic problems to solve" (1992: 6). Paul Martin echoed identical sentiments in his inaugural budget address: "Tough times test more than our patience and our pocket-books, they test our values and our worth" (1994: 19). In 1991 Michael Wilson expressed a degree of regret at the measures of his budget, a budget that centralized the debt issue: "Without a doubt, this is the most difficult of the seven budgets I have presented. Particularly so because of the painful economic circumstances facing Canadians today" (1991: 4). Just a year earlier Wilson had aired the same theme: "The expenditure control measures in this budget are tough. They reflect the fact that after several years of restraint, there are no painless ways to cut spending" (1990: 11).

Tough times require courage and bravery. A *Globe and Mail* editorial from 25 June 1994 titled "Of debt, separatism and interest rates" sketches these themes: "The government [Ottawa] should act first. In light of international anxiety, it should announce new targets for deficit reduction, backed by *tougher* constraints on public spending. It should understand that *hard choices* cannot wait for the social policy review and the next budget.

Only *boldness* now can restore confidence" (emphasis added). Fear or hesitation is deemed inappropriate to the debt crisis. The CBC's *Prime Time News*, in its budgetary preview on 21 February 1994, opened with a clip of Paul Martin: "This is no time to be timid nor traditional. We have got to move beyond the crude budgetary practices of a cut here or a trim there." Pamela Wallin, the host of the news program, then posed the inevitable question: "Well, tomorrow is Budget Day, and we will find out which course Paul Martin has chosen in his first budget." A *Globe and Mail* editorial from 16 May 1994 extolling the merits of the Klein government in Alberta puts the matter very bluntly: "A phenomenon has emerged in Alberta. Mr. Klein is doing what *other politicians have always been afraid to do*: cut actual spending and programs that people really value" (A12, emphasis added). The C.D. Howe Institute implicitly assesses the source of Canada's fiscal failure with a multi-authored publication pointedly and revealingly entitled *The Courage to Act* (1994). Another *Globe and Mail* editorial, in response to Paul Martin's inaugural budget, accuses him of "cowardice" (23 February 1994: A20). By the next year, however, the *Globe and Mail* reaches the conclusion that Martin has overcome his temerity: "Too little, too late? Too harsh. Better to say just enough, for now. But Canadians, and those abroad who wish us well, must hope that this *brave* beginning, so long delayed, will now be sustained" (emphasis added). The *Globe's* 30 April 1991 assessment of Floyd Laughren, the NDP minister of finance in Ontario, was somewhat less charitable: "If treasurers are to be in a position to help the economy along during a recession, they must have enough *iron in their spine* to toughly control spending when it is over. Mr. Laughren, it seems, does not have the necessary determination, and the people of Ontario will certainly pay the bill" (A14, emphasis added).

Not surprisingly, the centrality of these themes invites overt military parlance. The Business Council on National Issues, in its *A Ten Point Growth and Employment Strategy for Canada* released in the late summer of 1994, represents the challenge regarding Canada's debt as a parrying exercise against the "daggers aimed at the heart of Canada." The daggers will "find their mark unless *bold measures* are taken quickly to restore order to the country's public finances" (emphasis added). Similarly, Tom d'Aquino's address to the Rotary Club of Ottawa in January 1986 forefronted the gendered underbrush regarding bravery and militarism: "Some of the least responsible members of our society will persist in calling for not smaller deficits and leaner governments, but more of everything. The Prime Minister, Minister of Finance, and the Cabinet as a whole, must soldier on, nevertheless. In this battle, our political generals must lead the charge" (20 January 1986: 10).

The war on debt demands that people make sacrifices. The only question that emerges concerns efforts to make sure that these sacrifices are shared equally by all. Observe the following exchange between Pamela Wallin and Paul Martin on the CBC's *Prime Time News* in 22 February 1994:

Wallin:    The other group that feels a bit under attack tonight, Mr. Martin, is seniors in this country, people over the age of 65. You intend to take $300 million out of their pockets over the course of the next two years. There seems to be so many other loopholes and places for you to get that kind of money, why people over the age of 65?

Martin:    Seventy-five per cent of all seniors are not touched at all by that measure [a budgetary measure making age tax credits contingent upon income]. It's only those who are above $25,000, and the only people who lose it completely are those who are at the $50,000 level.

Wallin:    But Mr. Martin, people living on $25,000 a year in cities across the country are living well below the poverty line.

Martin:    And the amount of money we took away is very, very small. . . . What we've said is we have a deficit, and everybody has to put their shoulder to the wheel, and the only way that people are going to think they're dealt with fairly is that if everybody sees that everybody else is getting hit a little bit.

For this discussion, the idea that sacrifice must be spread around is more important than the finance minister's admission that 75 per cent of all seniors live below the poverty line. Business also has picked up on this idea of sharing the sacrifice. As Tom D'Aquino stated in the winter of 1986: "Business, the beneficiary of about 12 percent of federal program spending, must bear its share of the burden. The abundant selective tax measures that benefit business—the tax exemptions, deductions, credits, reduced tax rates and tax deferrals—must be subject to tough scrutiny and to sizeable cuts. Industrial subsidies and grants to business, some of dubious value, must also be pared down" (20 January 1986).

There is, in the end, a constant reiteration of firmness and resolve. There is a tough job in need of doing, and indecisiveness, caution, hesitation, weakness or poor resolve—things that are typically attributed to the feminine side of life—are deemed to be inadequate for the task at hand. "We have said from the beginning that we would meet our targets," stressed Paul

Martin in his 1995 budget address, "come what may" (1995: 3). A year earlier Martin cautioned Canadians "not to rush" but rather to "get things right" with respect to fiscal matters, and immediately added: "But make no mistake. There will be change" (1994: 3). A line has been drawn in the fiscal sands.

## The Loss of Control

A number of rudimentary aspects of gendered life coalesce around the idea of control and the fear of its loss. For instance, the masculine ethos is replete with ideas of mastery, including the valorization of self-mastery, a determination to be master over the body (with the body linked to womanliness) and mastery over nature (with nature also being interpreted as woman). Indeed, the drive to master nature has been identified as a central idea in the development of modern Western science (Keller 1985). The theme of mastery is complemented by ideas of independence and autonomy. Preserving independence is the ethos of masculinity. Masculine identity is permeated with notions of independence and disconnectedness. These ideas undergird the tendency to divide the world into parts, and promote the development of attendant intellectual baggage through concepts such as sovereignty. Consequently, the emergence of conditions of dependence and the loss of autonomy are suggestive of masculine erosion or decay and are associated with a gravitation towards the feminine. These salient dimensions of gendered life *inter alia* combine to associate manliness with control. In short, a good man is one who stays in control, who stays in command of difficult situations and who does not succumb to emotional lapses. Put baldly, it is better to be in control (more manly) than to be out of control (more womanly). The articulation of events or developments as threats to control identifies them as obviously serious.

The discourse of fiscal crisis is threaded with fear and concern about the loss of control. Government spending is represented frequently as being "out of control." Successive proclamations of fiscal restraint followed by higher deficits, especially at the federal level, have added to this widespread sense. In an interview on CBC's *The Journal* on 26 February 1991 by Barbara Frum of Michael Wilson this idea was put pointedly to the finance minister: "Let me ask you about the debt, because some people will hear you again fighting the deficit and meanwhile it's gone outside of your control once again, and say, hey, this is *déjà vu* all over again, you haven't got control of this process." A *Globe and Mail* editorial from 17 November 1993 expresses a similar concern with a loss of control. "Extrapolating from the first six months of the current fiscal year produces a deficit of $45 billion. It probably won't be that bad, of course, but then on previous form it's at least as likely to be worse. The 1992–93 figure, recall, was reckoned at $34 billion this time last year, which was already well in excess of the budget's target of $27.5 billion. Oops. This ought to persuade anyone that federal finances are, in the most literal sense, out of control" (A18). Again, at the conclusion of his 1990 budget address Michael Wilson summed up the goal of his budgetary measures: "Indeed, if we maintain our resolve, the prospect of low inflation is within sight, and we have the deficit under firm control."

Part of the concern with the loss of control is expressed through the idea of "debt drift." This idea conjures up the image of fiscal aimlessness or lack of direction, not unlike a boat that has lost its power at sea. A C.D. Howe Institute publication entitled *Paying Our Way: The Welfare State in Hard Times,* is introduced by John Richards, a frequent contributor to the Institute's publications, as part of a political strategy to "break with the conventions of 'debt drift.'" Richards adds that "the essays in this volume conclude that continued 'debt drift' poses uncertain, but potentially severe, economic, political, and social problems" (1994: xi). As Paul Martin echoed at the outset of his first budget speech: "The days of government simply nibbling at the edges are over. The practice of endless process without product is gone. Our task is to put an end to drift" (1994: 1).

The emphasis on securing control of Canadian finances routinely appears in ways that are suggestive of manhood being challenged or weakened: "there is a new harsh reality that has completely altered the function of budgets and the fiscal policies they reflect. There was a time," Peter C. Newman wrote in Maclean's in 4 March 1991, "when budgets were creative fiscal instruments, allowing finance ministers to shape the economy, nudging one sector while holding back another—helping to fine tune the tricky balance between inflation and recession. . . . But [now] his discretionary power of making a significant impact on the Canadian economy are on a par with Joe Clark's ability to terrify Saddam Hussein" (46).

Finally, the concern with control extends to Canada's relationship with global economic institutions or foreign money lenders. The amount of the debt held in foreign hands is often presented as lessening Canadian control over the debt. The possibility that policy control might be lost to institutions such as the International Monetary Fund (IMF) if Canada loses access to credit is expressed frequently. A *Globe and Mail* editorial from 16 May 1995 makes the point rather bluntly: "It is simply fatuous to suggest that there is any question of where sovereignty lies. Discretion in making economic policy erodes only if a country so mismanages its sovereign affairs that it loses its credit in world markets . . . and has to ask the IMF to come in to supervise until its credibility is regained. Sovereignty cannot be taken; it can only be given away" (A16).

## The Economy in Abstract Terms

Patriarchal consciousness identifies abstraction as a prototypical masculine faculty. Qualities associated with thought and thinking, including the mind, rationality, reason and abstraction, are intertwined with understandings of masculinity. In rather dramatic contrast, the feminine side of patriarchal consciousness is associated with intuition, concreteness, emotion and the body. Entire intellectual spheres of culture, especially philosophy, appear in novel ways when presented in terms of this consonance with rudimentary aspects of masculinity. In patriarchal culture, the framing of problems abstractly, or refusing steadfastly to characterize problems in terms of their bodily or concrete human dimensions, is intuited generally as a positive development. The difficulties created by this cultural reflex have been decried in the past. As one nineteenth century writer stresses with respect to reflections on the economy in particular, analysts are remiss if their contemplative activities cause them to overlook "practical, human-sensuous activity."

The discourse of fiscal crisis invariably represents economic activity and fiscal policy in purely abstract terms. This is a world of reserves net of lapse, deficit to GDP ratio, debt to GDP ratio, open economy, marginal product, nominal growth, real growth, and so on. One of the most talked about statistics concerns the debt to GDP ratio. The economic evolution of this ratio, for example, received the following treatment: "The ratio of debt to GDP evolves according to a very simple relationship: specifically, if X denotes to debt-to-GDP ratio, and the subscripts $a$ and $b$ denote "this year" and "last year," respectively then $X_a = (1 + r - g) \times X_b + \text{noninterest deficit/GDP}_a$, where r is the real rate of interest and g is the growth rate of real GDP. One can quickly see," the author adds, "the crucial relationship that the real interest rate plays relative to the real growth rate" (Harris 1994: 24). The problem here is not one of difficulty or accessability. Rather, it lies in the manner in which such representations mystify the human side of productive life. As abstractions they have little to do with daily living. They insulate discussants from considering the human effects of their policy recommendations, and inure them to criticism, especially criticism regarding the human consequences of their recommendations.

The discourse of fiscal crisis is constructed through this pervasive tendency to speak about the economy in purely abstract terms. This allows analysts to avoid discussions that focus upon the human side of fiscal policy. People, to the extent that they are addressed at all, appear as tax-payers, welfare recipients, seasonal workers and so forth. It is not appropriate to speak of the debt's concrete human dimensions, especially the hardship and uncertainty created by the reduction of government spending or the life styles of the bond holders. In the context of the discourse it would not be appropriate to muse about the hardening of children's stools because of declining affordability of dietary roughage in an era of cutbacks. To speak about the debt in terms of access to cold and flu medication or the affordability of meat exceeds the boundaries of the discourse. Considering the economy in terms of sexual harassment on the job gets eclipsed. In the end, the only permissible way of speaking about the economy is without regard to people. The only way to be heard, to avoid being marginalized or to be taken seriously is to remain aloof to lived life.

Occasionally, an unease with the discourse's disregard for lived human experiences and detachment from the hardships of daily life creeps into discussions about debt management. In a CBC *Prime Time News* panel discussion following the 1995 budget, for example, Nancy Riche of the Canadian Labour Congress emphasized that "we [Canadian Labour] lost tonight 45,000 jobs. These are people. These are not 'civil servants' and numbers" (27 February 1995). This particular discussion, predictably, immediately returned to the idea of unwieldy government. The boundaries of the discourse had been transgressed. A CBC *Prime Time News* panel discussion from 4 February 1994 provides an excellent illustration of the fact that the margins of a discourse are not policed perfectly. During the discussion Lloyd Axworthy, Liberal minister of human resources, be-moaned that fact that deficit cutting measures overlook people: "When I go into the House of Commons, I'm faced with an opposition that says, how much are you giving to the provinces? And I come out, and the journalists are sort of saying, how are you cutting social programs? They never ask, how does that program affect the individual woman with a child? We've got the debate all wrong." Melanie Hess of the Canadian Council on Social Development immediately underscored Axworthy's exceptional observations by adding to the discussion: "that's what worries me because I think the human dimension is lost in the shuffle here." These reflections attest to the absence of something very fundamental. If they were to be sustained it would signal a fundamental shift in the debt discourse itself. Not surprisingly, the program moderator immediately transposed these observations into a question about which level of government should deliver social programs in Canada.

## The Reasonableness of Fiscal Restraint

The discourse of fiscal crisis stands on its proclaimed reasonableness. This is especially true for its policy prescriptions regarding state spending in an era of ballooning debts. Reason is a powerful card in the context of patriarchal culture. That is, in the dichotomous world of gender, reason is associated directly with masculinity while its absence—manifested espe-cially through the idea of emotion—is associated with notions of womanliness. To be reasonable is to be manly; to be emotional is to be womanly. The quality of reason is undergirded, in turn, by simple binaries of gender including mind/body and thought/intuition. In effect, the idea of reason is knitted so tightly with the idea of manliness that women pursuing traditional fields such as philosophy could be put in a very perplexing situation: "For a woman to love Reason," writes Sara Ruddick in her studies of maternal thought and practices, "was to risk both self-contempt and a self-alienating misogyny" (Ruddick 1989: 5). In effect, to endow a quality or a perspective with reason is to imbue it with masculine qualities which are inevitably valued in the context of masculinist society.

The prevailing representation of the debt discourse is that it exclusively occupies reasonable space; it is the only reasonable way to think about debt issues. The discourse of fiscal crisis is the distillation or product of reason. It is the necessary product of the activity of thought. A *Globe and Mail* editorial from 12 October 1994 entitled "The new math," in response to claims that unemployment insurance (UI) ledgers should not be included in calculations of annual federal deficits, provides an example of this aspect of the debt discourse. The editorial argues that Canada's fiscal situation is bleaker, not better, due to the fact that interest payments as a proportion of federal revenues appear more burdensome if UI revenues are excluded. The conclusion of the editorial is telling: "Of course. Not all news is bad news, but this editorial certainly is. Sorry, it's the damn, damning math" (A20). As Paul Martin declared in his 1995 budget speech: "The debt and deficit are not inventions of ideology. They are facts of arithmetic. The quicksand of compound interest is *real*" (1995: 2).

This claim of reasonableness is sometimes made through common metaphors such as lightness and darkness. A 27 March 1995 *Globe and Mail* editorial, celebrating the cost-cutting measures of the Wells government in Newfoundland, begins as follows: "It may be as faint as a fogbound morning in Bonavista, but there is a new light in Newfoundland" (A10). In response to the release of the Canadian Centre for Policy Alternatives's *Bleeding the Patient*, a publication that attacks the deficit fighting measures of the federal government, a *Globe and Mail* editorial from 11 May 1993 observes that a dispute has erupted between those on the left who accept the policy exigencies created by the debt crisis and those who continue to attack the idea that there is a debt crisis. It describes the two supposed camps on the left as a struggle between "those who have been forced by experience in office or the weight of evidence to acknowledge the bankruptcy of their beliefs, and those who simply refuse. While their compatriots stumble, blinking, toward the light, their response is to retreat still further into the dark, railing at the treachery of the departed and consoling themselves with tales of conspiracy and evil spirits" (A18).

On other occasions, the declaration that the prevailing debt discourse is reasonable is pressed much more straightforwardly: "Reasonable people can differ on whether deficits, in a small open economy, stimulate anything but bond traders. But no one, we hope, argues that it is a legitimate policy goal to run deficits each and every year, without regard to the state of the business cycle, the uses to which such borrowing is put, or the ability of future generations to carry it" (*Globe and Mail* 11 May 1993: A18). An early publication of the C.D. Howe Institute reproduces the reason/emotion dichotomy to make the same point: "We want to carefully distinguish what we believe are sound reasons for concerns about the government deficit from the emotive views that are often expressed" (Bruce and Purvis 1984: 5–6). On other occasions the claim of reasonableness is made through related language. As Tom d'Aquino claimed in 23 February 1989, deficit fighting "is the cause of responsibility and common sense" (11). As a last example, in his 1992 budget speech, Don Mazankowski drew upon ideas of reasonableness: "Times are difficult. There are serious economic problems to solve. But there is no substitute for sound policies. That is the realistic perspective in which this budget was developed" (1992: 6).

To quarrel with the basic ideas of the dominant debt narrative is to flirt with unreason or *to be* unreasonable. It is especially this dimension of the debt discourse that creates a powerful justification for neo-liberal policies. The neo-liberal policy agenda, an agenda that largely is commensurate with the policy prescriptions of the discourse of fiscal crisis, appears as the only reasonable option. Consequently, a politically charged and socially harmful policy agenda surfaces as the only reasonable set of options. This casting is a powerful device. When the neo-liberal policy program convincingly presents itself as the only reasonable option because the state is "broke," it goes a long way towards consolidating its consensual foundation across class lines.

Moreover, dissenting discourses and policy prescriptions *ipso facto* appear as unreasonable. Policy proposals that advocate increases in government spending, for example, are shut down. In effect, any political project that seeks to enlist the state in its cause comes to appear unreasonable when it advocates increases in financial support or when it decries funding cuts. Political groups that continue to press for funding support tend to be cast as cavalier and irresponsible. Similarly, activists who condemn government cutbacks because of their harmful effects upon welfare recipients, single mothers or the disabled are dismissed as advocates of "special interests," a term calling attention to their refusal to accept the reasonableness of fiscal restraint on behalf of the entire social body.

In effect, politics becomes reincarnated as a process of fiscal management defined by the logic of the debt crisis, debt walls and the looming paralysis of government services. The political, conceived at least in part in terms of a struggle to enlist the state on behalf of groups responding to the contradictions and dislocations associated with contemporary capitalist society, is bullied into submission. Any broader sense of politics as a clash among competing visions of the future is silenced as well. Expressed somewhat facetiously, how can there be a serious discussion about alternative futures in the face of so much reason?

## The Authoritative Voice

The voice of authority is integral to the masculine side of patriarchal consciousness. For the expression of opinions and the relaying of information to be manly, it must proceed in an assured, confident manner. The masculine voice commands attention and respect. Conversely, the feminine dimension of patriarchal culture struggles to be heard and, perhaps even more importantly, to be received seriously. Moreover, there is a very subtle ideology of seriousness that feeds into the cultivation of authority; it demands gravity over frivolity, controlled voices over enthusiastic outbursts, stern physiognomies over relaxed expressions, solemnity, dark apparel and an imposing posture.

The truths of the discourse of fiscal crisis are unassailable and the conveyance is parental. First the fiscal truths. Owing significantly to its abstraction and it claims of reasonableness, an air of credibility is achieved by the hegemonic discourse. The identification of the debt as a crisis and its specific cost-cutting solutions achieve the status of mathematical truths. A sort of scientific aura has emerged, one that lends an air of authority and irrefutability to claims about the debt. The debt discourse, in effect, reads off the Logos of economic science. The conveyors of debt information simply give voice to truths—the term "debt realism" has emerged recently —discerned by experts who, it should be noted, are typically male; their victims, not incidentally, especially as revealed through statistics on poverty, are predominantly female. In view of this, institutions such as bond rating agencies, pundits from the financial community, finance ministers and business-supported groups such as the BCNI or the Fraser Institute are not viewed as representing a perspective—one that might support certain fractions of capital or the interests of money lenders, for instance. These prevailing representations of the debt issue imbue otherwise highly contentious, politically loaded claims with an objective status.

These apparent truths are conveyed in an assured and authoritative manner. The debt is *discussed*, but never *discussed lightly*. It is not laughed about; it is not a casual concern. The public is positioned to receive information like children in the lap of their parents. Warnings about the deteriorating fiscal situation or announcements of further government cuts are conveyed in the manner of a reluctant parent about to discipline a child;

they remind one of the "this is going to hurt me more that it will hurt you" experiences of childhood. "My message today," ruefully declared Michael Wilson as he released his budget in 1986, "is a serious one and in many ways not pleasant" (1986: 1).

## Conclusion

Why does the discourse of fiscal crisis ring true despite its highly contentious elements? Why have its basic premises been accepted so widely? Why is it so alluring and convincing? As this chapter has argued, much of its persuasive power can be found in its accordance with patriarchal consciousness. It is sensible and convincing by virtue of the fact that the discourse is informed by the intuitive fabric of patriarchy, particularly with respect to its concern about bravery and sacrifice, its express fear about losing control, its inherent abstraction, its identification with reasonableness and its air of authority. It was, in a sense, inevitable that the discourse of fiscal crisis would be constructed in this manner; at the same time its gendered elements remain its most powerful drawing card. Consonance with the masculine in a masculinist society tends to fly. A debt discourse that simply disregarded the idea of sacrifice would be received with greater difficulty. A debt discourse that concerned itself with the stresses of living in an age of welfare rollbacks or one that presented itself as an emotional response to the threat of foreign money lenders would have much less credibility. Indeed, the disciplining mechanisms directing us away from things intuited as feminine during the formative stages of the discourse would tend to foreclose these possibilities.

As a concluding illustration, a *Globe and Mail* editorial from 8 February 1995 which expresses concern with the pace of social assistance reform in an era of fiscal crisis draws many of these gendered themes together. Entitled "Canada, Land of Oz," it inveighs against the pace of the Liberal policy review with references to characters from the *Wizard of Oz* : "In conceiving reform, for example, the government was the Straw Man. It has no analysis and no rationale. . . . When Mr. Axworthy's green paper preceded rather than followed Paul Martin's economic statement last fall, it missed a chance to tie social programs to the deficit" (A18). The editorial continues: "In announcing reform, the government was the Tin Man. It never had the heart for reform because too few Liberals embraced it. They were unconvinced that it was needed primarily to save money." It concludes: "In executing reform, the government was the Lion. Even if it had found the argument and heart, it lacked the courage to act." The discourse of fiscal crisis clearly informs this editorial, and its elements of abstraction, reasonableness and courage in particular imbue the editorial's argumentative line with an inherent commonsensibility.

CHAPTER FIVE

# INDIVIDUAL RESPONSIBILITY AND THE DISCOURSE OF FISCAL CRISIS

The discourse of fiscal crisis is replete with ideas informed by understandings of the individual and individual responsibility. These ideas draw upon common assumptions about the role and nature of the individual within contemporary capitalist society in the West. The debt discourse is, therefore, consonant with an age where each person has been isolated philosophically—as epitomized in the liberal problematic that pits an individual against other individuals and against the state. The isolation also takes a practical form, especially through the dissolution of traditional forms of community due to the commodification of life and the fractionation of work.

Underlying these developments has been the growing need for working people to be mobile. For most, the only available option in contemporary capitalist society is to sell their labour power. Increasingly, people must travel in search of work. Everything from economic downturns to increased capital mobility makes it more difficult to secure a job "at home." Working people do not have the option of staying close to home, in the old neighbourhood or near their home town. Movement has become the norm. In Canada, it is common to move from one province to another, from one region to another or from the rural areas to the urban centres. Small-scale and large-scale migration of labour has intensified in the post-Second World War era. Consequently, in addition to the destruction of the foundation of traditional communities, there is a disintegration of families and extended families. It is noteworthy, for example, that telephone companies are able to reference these common situations to sell their services. This also helps to explain the appeal to ideas about family and community that now, ironically, constitute a significant portion of corporate advertising. The dissolution of traditional forms of community has been exacerbated by the growing separation of people from friends and family, especially at the level of daily contact.

During these developments greater responsibility falls onto individuals. Daily routines are no longer shared within the family or community. Rather, each person must attend to their personal needs or those of their immediate family. In all spheres of life, to employ a common expression, people are "on their own." Families, extended families, friends and communities are less likely to be there to lend a hand. A helpful example here concerns the changing nature of homework in the last century. While it conventionally has been deemed "women's work," a fact that continues to this day, the nature of homework has become more onerous. All the gadgets in the world cannot make up for the fact that women now undertake work in the home without help or relief from other women. Mothers, grandmothers or sisters are less likely to be close enough to assist regularly.

These changing realities have been attended by the cultivation of a powerful sense of individual responsibility over the last century in the West. There has been the creation of a culture of self-reliance. People are expected to take care of themselves. Reliance upon others is viewed increasingly with disdain. Individuals must manage their own affairs and provide for themselves. The widespread view is that responsibility for shelter, food, parenting, financial management, work and so forth all fall to the individual rather than the family or community. More recently, even the elderly are expected to attend to themselves, at least financially, as the increasingly common practice of establishing retirement savings plans confirms. The failure to provide for these things, and to do so well, invites scorn and contempt. To "live off " someone else is assessed harshly.

The discourse of fiscal crisis draws directly upon two elements that form part of the culture of self-reliance. The first element concerns the management of personal finances. That is, an analogy is drawn between individual finances and those of the state. The importance of managing state finances properly is analogized to personal finances in an age of unprecedented credit and consumption. Hence, state fiscal policy must be carried out in a manner that accords with personal financial management. The comparison allows responsible state policy to be assessed according to the same powerful understandings that are associated with personal responsibility.

The second element the fiscal crisis discourse draws on is the understanding that individuals on social assistance have failed in some way; their "failure" is usually conveyed through the idea that they have become dependent upon social assistance or welfare. The inclination to attack recipients of state assistance has intensified as they have become causally linked to the fiscal difficulties through the prevailing debt discourse.

## The Analogy to Personal Finances

The discourse of fiscal crisis draws upon widely appreciated and understood aspects of personal financing. The basic dimension of these common experiences is straightforward. Briefly, each person in society receives some sort of income or revenue and is forced to make expenditures. This is owing directly to the extension of the commodity form to most goods and services in society. Most income goes towards the purchase of necessities, such as food and housing. Extra income might be saved or spent on non-essentials. (The distinction between essentials and non-essentials is somewhat fluid. A television was once viewed as a luxury. This is no longer the case.) Regardless of levels of disposable income, however, individuals can purchase goods and services on credit. The availability of credit has grown exponentially over the last three decades. Everything from homes to vacations to lawn mowers can now be purchased through credit. This development has added monthly interest charges to an individual's expenses.

As every individual knows, some sort of equilibrium must be maintained between income and expenditures (necessities, non-essentials and interest payments). The cost of discharging one's debts (principal plus interest), along with other necessary outlays of money, cannot exceed one's total income for any sustained period of time. In the short term this often happens. Individuals often will delay or miss monthly credit card payments. Worse still, they might forgo essentials, especially food, to meetly their monthly credit payments. Short-term credit arrears are a very common practice. When this situation occurs, credit ratings deteriorate (one of the principal leverages against individual debtors) and further credit becomes unavailable. Deteriorating credit ratings are intuited widely as an unfortunate personal development. If the process is sustained for any length of time a sort of personal financial crisis emerges. Individuals will scramble to borrow from family members or financial institutions. Consolidation of credit payments through a bank loan is a common practice. Failing this, however, individuals can lose their access to credit very quickly. Ultimately, individuals might be forced to declare personal bankruptcy, that is, admit publicly that they are unable to discharge their credit payments in exchange for varying degrees of immunity from creditors.

This basic process is universally understood. Great care is taken not to damage credit ratings. Equally great care is taken not to over-extend oneself in terms of credit. Most people learn the principle of managing credit. Going into debt is all right, as long as the debt is serviceable. People do not get into credit trouble intentionally. Moreover, the ability to manage personal finances to avoid personal bankruptcy is valued highly. Declarations of personal bankruptcy are associated with carelessness and profligacy.

The discourse of fiscal crisis extends the scenario of personal finance to the state. A brief review of budget speeches reveals this clearly. In 1992 the federal finance minister stressed that the budgetary measures were to discipline governments in the same manner that all other areas of society had been disciplined: "All these measures respond to a clear message from Canadians: difficult times are no excuse for governments to live beyond the taxpayers' means. It has not been business-as-usual for thousands of Canadian taxpayers, farmers, fishermen, business people, workers and families. It cannot be business-as-usual for any government that truly cares." In short, government must "adjust to the same budget realities that households and businesses must face every day" (Mazankowski 1992: 6). As Bill Robson, the C.D. Howe Institute's unselfconscious debt guru, stressed on a segment of CBC's *Prime Time News* Magazine on 21 February 1994, with respect to Canada's borrowing practices, "when you borrow, you have to pay interest on the debt. It's straight forward. Every family knows that. . . ." The idea that Canadian fiscal policy must respond to its "pocketbook," that is, to something colloquially understood as an income/expense ledger for individuals, is very common. "We need to redesign the role of the government in the economy," stressed Paul Martin in his second budget address, "to fit the size of our pocketbook and the priorities of our people" (1995: 7). Martin later added: "Canadians make ends meet by watching their dollar every day. It's time government did the same" (ibid.: 15).

The idea of "affordability" is presented in terms of issues not unlike those that would face individuals and households deciding on their financial ability to purchase a new car. In his first budget, for example, Paul Martin stated that "for years, governments have been promising more than they can deliver, and delivering more that they can afford" (1994: 2). Most budget addresses reiterate the same idea. "How did Canada acquire this enormous debt? Well, like any family or individual might have done," retorted Michael Wilson in 1989, "Canada did it by living beyond its means" (1989: 1). In the end, one of the most common ideas in the discourse of fiscal crisis is the notion of getting the "government's fiscal house in order." A similar notion of "belt-tightening" can often be heard. This is a particularly callous idea that trivializes the increasing hardship faced by many individuals and families throughout Canada society. The proliferation of food banks is a clear indicator of this trend.

That government financing is similar to individual financing is a common refrain. As C.D. Howe economist Irene Ip declared in 1993,

"Canadians don't realize that they are like people who live off their credit card and eventually have to face the music" (McMurdy 1993). The Conservative party, prior to its devastating defeat in the 1993 election, evinced the same refrain. In a 27 September 1993 election speech in Surrey, B.C., then Prime Minister Kim Campbell remarked that "governments face the same reality that you do in your daily lives. You can't spend money that you don't have. If you borrow money, you have to repay it. Most importantly, you must make sure that you don't have to borrow money regularly, especially if you can't repay it without borrowing even more." Campbell refined her analogy with a more direct reference to personal finances: "This country has racked up a Visa bill that is so large that we have to borrow money just to pay the interest on that national Visa bill."

A *Maclean's* article from May 1993 draws upon the comparison as a way of describing the task facing Don Mazankowski, the Progressive Conservative minster of finance. "Once he was a small-town car salesman. Now, still in his 50s," the article analogizes, "he is the chief financial officer of the country's largest employer, delivering his fiscal plan to a cash-strapped organization" (Blythe, Allen, Fisher and Wood 1993: 10). On an earlier occasion *Maclean's* also compared a small business with the finance portfolio: "As a boy, Donald Mazankowski liked nothing better than to stand behind the cash register of a rural Alberta hardware store. . . . Nearly half a century and 2,740 kilometres removed from the prairie town, Mazankowski is now in charge of the biggest—and most dramatically empty—cash register in the country."

A Reform Party document from 1993, entitled *Stop Digging!: A Presentation of the Reform Party's Plan to Reduce the Federal Deficit to Zero in Three Years*, provides an excellent example of the operation of the analogy to personal finances. It begins by situating the reader or listener in a restaurant. At the outset of the document the reader is told to imagine that she or he has just finished a fine meal. "Just imagine that the dinner is over, the last coffees have been poured, and the waiter brings the bill." Thus, the reader is asked to conjure up an experience that is widely shared. At this point, however, the customer/reader suddenly discovers that she or he is unable to pay for the meal. "You have no cash, so you give the waiter your credit card," the document observes, "but he comes back and says you are over your credit limit. You try to write a cheque, but the waiter won't accept it" (1). The situation is easy to imagine. It draws upon common experiences in a credit-laden age. Other images arise such as depositing an expensive watch or working the meal off by toiling in the kitchen—the stuff of many comedic premises. The document stresses that the sort of fear and desperation that one would feel when faced with the inability to cover the costs of a meal, especially after availing oneself of the restaurant's services, is exactly like the anxiety that international bankers and investors feel when they look at Canada's debt. "It's rather like the panic you would feel if you suddenly found yourself unable to pay for the wonderful dinner you had just eaten at a city restaurant, after having been encouraged and invited to take whatever you want from the menu" (1). In sum, the opening of *Stop Digging!* likens financial concern over the debt to a situation that many people understand (and have possibly experienced directly).

## Living Beyond Its Means

The idea that state finances are like personal finances is often expressed through the idea of "living within one's means." Like individuals in late twentieth century capitalism, the state must maintain some sort of equilibrium between revenue and expenditures. If the state borrows money, then it is held that the cost of servicing this debt (paying interest and sometimes principal) along with regular expenditures cannot exceed total collected revenues. Just like individuals, the state should only allow itself to be "in the red" for a relatively short period of time. "It is not necessary—or appropriate—for the federal government's revenue to match spending exactly in every year," confirms a 1989 C.D. Howe publication entitled *Building a Constituency for Deficit Reduction*, "any more than it is necessary for an individual to earn every dollar that he or she spends in a year." Debts must always remain manageable. The state should not allow its costs of debt servicing to continually expand in proportion to its overall revenue raising capacities. This would cause the state's credit rating to fall (courtesy of international bond-rating agencies such as Moody's or Standard and Poores). To sell its bonds the state would have to offer higher interest rates, effectively costing it more to borrow money. This would exacerbate the state's precarious financial position by raising its debt servicing costs, creating a debt spiral. Ultimately, the state, as international confidence fell, could find itself in a position where international lenders refused it money, not unlike the situation of an individual being turned down by a bank when applying for a loan. The state would be hitting the debt wall. Essentially, it would be broke or bankrupt.

The Canadian government is frequently accused of "living beyond its means." This accusation conjures up images of a profligate, irresponsible individual who racks up credit card debts and suddenly finds herself or himself in a situation where she or he can no longer make minimum payments. In his post-budget interview with Pamela Wallin on the CBC's *Prime Time News* on 27 February 1995, for example, Paul Martin expressed this theme with pith: "We really felt that Canadians live within their means, why shouldn't government."

A common theme that draws upon the idea of "living within one's means" is the notion that state borrowing in the context of ever-expanding debt-servicing costs is like "mortgaging the future." A *Globe and Mail* editorial from 9 November 1992 entitled "Bleak House" draws upon many aspects of personal financing to illustrate this idea. It begins by bemoaning the fact that the idea of mortgaging the future has become banal: "This is a shame, because the phrase ['mortgaging our future'] describes with almost literal precision how successive governments have undermined the nation's finances." At this point the editorial asks the reader to conjure up the typical situation between a home owner and a renter: "Picture Canada as a house, and the federal government as the homeowner (sorry: in this metaphor," the editorial added parenthetically, "ordinary Canadians are mere tenants.) In 1969, the home owner had a manageable mortgage of $18-billion, the size of the national debt at the time. His family accounts, the federal budget, showed a slight surplus of $300,000. So the prospects of eventually paying off the mortgage—the dream of every Canadian homeowner—seemed good." After reviewing the spending proclivities of the Liberal governments from 1970 through to 1985, the editorial observes, "to pay for all this spending, the government, in effect, took out second, third and fourth mortgages." The editorial then accounts for the change in government by continuing the analogy: "In September, 1984, the house changed hands with the election of a new Conservative government. Realizing that things could not go on the way they had, the new homeowner did two things: limit the amount it was spending on the operation and maintenance of the house [analogized to Canada's social and economic infrastructure] and sharply raised the rent for the tenants [analogized to tax increases]." The editorial then turns to its basic point, namely, that the Tory government was not "zealous" enough in its spending cuts. "As a result," the editorial continues, "we have not been able even to think about paying off the mortage." As the title of the editorial suggests, the situation is dismal: "If this really were a house, the tenants would have moved out long ago and the bank would have repossessed the property. But it's a country. Lenders like countries. They know that the tenants cannot leave and that the landowner can compel them to pay any rent increase. Oh, there might be a tax revolt—but against whom. In the end, there is only ourselves" (A14).

A similar idea is presented with more flare in an editorial article, "If We Care About People," released by the Canadian Chamber of Commerce. It asks: "What is the debt, anyway? It's a mortage on Canada." It then elaborates on this idea: "For years, governments have borrowed money, and put up our country for collateral. Now they are borrowing money to pay the interest—this is the deficit. That's like putting your own mortgage payments on your credit card. It's just common sense. Pretty soon our credit is going to run out. And [just like a family that loses its home due to a mortgage foreclosure] we could lose everything." The editorial then dramatizes the size of Canada's debt by continuing the analogy: "How big is this mortgage? More than half a trillion dollars. That many loonies would circle the earth 317 times, cross the entire country coast-to-coast 1,780 times, or line Canada's shores 52 times. If the government started collecting one loonie from every Canadian every hour—that's 29 million loonies every hour—the mortgage would be paid off in two years" (n.d.: 1). As the chair of the Business Council on National Issues stated in the fall of 1994, "we are not paying our own way. You could say we're putting the tab for our present *high living* on our grandchildren's VISA cards" (emphasis added).

## Groundless Analogy

Of course, state finances bear little similarity to personal financing. Governments have, for example, a host of revenue-raising mechanisms at their disposal, especially in larger economies. Current governments have been reluctant to use their taxing power in response to various pressures, most notably from the middle classes that feel "taxed out" or from capital in the era of global restructuring. It is significant that levels of corporate taxation have fallen dramatically in the last two decades. This must be understood as a political choice on the part of governments. The global disciplining mechanisms that supposedly necessitate competitive taxation policies from country to country are greatly exaggerated. The composition of the tax burden is the product of cumulative political decisions, not the Logos of a globalizing world. Capital mobility is a costly thing for individual capitals, as was evident in Canada in the form of the concern raised by mid-sized capital over the free trade negotiations. Corporate taxation rates can be raised with relative impunity. Corporate tax waivers and deferrals are also under the immediate control of governments. In the end, just as the ratio of corporate income tax to all other taxes has shifted (in favour of capital) through political choices, so it can be turned back and then some. Simply put, taxation is still an option despite the claims and protestations that it is hazardous for economic growth and jobs—euphemisms for the real threat of falling profits which such taxation policies would pose for capital.

A second glaring reason why the analogy between state finances and personal finances cannot be sustained lies in the relationship between states and domestic and international financial systems. State debt is an integral part of that system. The extent of state borrowing (an ever-increasing practice) renders the financial community vulnerable to state-level defaults or debt cancellations. The financial community is always willing to roll over debts in the interest of systemic preservation. Other national governments, to add to this, are often willing to bail out financially troubled states in the interest of overall stability. "If you borrow a thousand dollars it is your problem," as one saying summarizes, "but if you borrow a million dollars, it becomes the bank's problem." Obviously, individuals do not pose a threat to the entire system and financial institutions will let them default. Nonetheless, states are very low-risk borrowers, and even the poorest states can find international lenders. In the parlance of the discourse of fiscal crisis, debt walls, for states, are hard to find, let alone hit.

A third conspicuous point that undermines the analogy between state finances and individual finances is the fact that individuals cannot control the cost of debt. Through their monetary policies states can control the cost of borrowing. Moreover, when central banks ease up on interest rates they can promote economic growth which, in turn, raises government revenues. Indeed, Canadian monetary policies have been implicated in the debt by a growing number of commentators, and constitute a central theme in many recent critiques including Linda McQuaig's *Shooting the Hippo* (1995).

A fourth limitation of the analogy between personal and state finances lies in the cyclical nature of government debt. Changes in the growth rates of economies affect yearly deficits. Slowdowns and contractions of the economy, if all other factors remain constant (especially with respect to tax laws and collection conventions), result in lower revenues for the state. Recessionary periods can wreak havoc on state accounts. The recent series of recessions in Canada since the onset of the mid-1970s crisis has exacerbated the profile of deficit years. That is, some deficits are unexpectedly high owing to lower than predicted revenues. Obviously, the undulations in the economy can have a significant impact on the level of government debt. This reality is very different for individuals. On an individual level there tends to be more stability in income (even though income levels will shift over the years). Moreover, expenditures and income can be equalized much more quickly on an individual level. Individuals also face a greater incentive to equalize expenditures and income by virtue of the reality of personal debt walls and spirals. In short, individuals tend not to experience unpredictable undulations in their personal income and, when they do their income/ expenditure ratios can be more easily balanced. In those situations where a family or an individual loses a source of income entirely (obviously a very serious situation and one that is occurring more frequently) personal financial crises arise quickly. Such a dramatic loss of income, however, would be more appropriately analogized to the complete collapse of the capitalist economy, something that has not yet happened.

In the end, there are no analytical grounds for drawing a comparison between individual finances and state finances. The analogy is accepted, certainly, but not grounded. Curiously, during the formative period of the discourse of fiscal crisis, economists regularly admitted this. As one C. D. Howe publication from 1984 noted, "a household . . . firm that continually borrows to finance current expenditure in excess of current receipts eventually goes bankrupt. It is often asserted that a similar fate awaits a government that tolerates large and persistent current deficits." However, the document then adds that "this analogy is misleading. Unlike households, the government does not have a finite lifetime over which its borrowing and lending must balance" (Bruce and Purvis 1984: 7).

The discourse once again draws upon popular understandings regardless of the veracity or accuracy of the analogy. The debt issue is cast with reference to the extensive personal experiences of everyone. The analogy, in a manner of speaking, makes sense. It is difficult to imagine an alternative reality of state finances that contradicts the widespread personal experiences of everyone. It is intuited in lieu of alternative practices or points of consciousness. In an age of unprecedented resort to personal credit the analogy is a powerful and effective device.

The comparison is integral to forging a consensual foundation for neo-liberalism. The manner in which the discourse of fiscal crisis plugs into personal experiences helps to explain why many people on fixed and low income support neo-liberal policies. A *Maclean's* article from 1 May 1989 "Where is the Deficit?" illustrates this well. It begins with the a very typical story about an elderly woman: "At the age of 16, Ruby Walsh quit school and took a job sewing burlap bags in a Nova Scotia sugar refinery to help support her family. Later, she married, raised two daughters and earned extra money selling Avon products and teaching dressmaking." An impression of a hard working, practical and responsible person is established. The story then shifts to the present: "Now approaching 70, a widow and a grandmother, Walsh lives in Dartmouth, N.S, on her monthly old-age pension cheques and the survivor benefits from her late husband." A very typical image of elderly persons has been created. The article then draws attention to her concerns regarding the possible reform of social policy: "But now, Walsh, who has been following the emotional debate over the federal budget deficit, says that she fears higher taxes and cuts in government services would make her life more difficult." The serious concern has the potential of undermining the prevailing debt discourse. However, the article immediately subdues any potential criticism by drawing upon the analogy to personal finances: "Still, as a self-reliant individual who always paid the family bills on time, she acknowledges the government's dilemma." It then quotes directly from Ruby Walsh: "'The money has to come from somewhere and the pot's empty. I just worry about cutting pensions.'" The article illustrates how individuals destined to be harmed by neo-liberal policies support it on the basis of the apparently sensible analogy to personal finances.

## The Cultivation of Anti-Welfarism

Closely related to the ideas of individual responsibility around personal financial matters are elements in the discourse of fiscal crisis that draw upon understandings relating to anti-welfare sentiments. A considerable portion of the debt is deemed to be the result of spending on programs for unmotivated or simply lazy members of society—people judged harshly in a culture of self-reliance. Government over-spending on individuals who do not make a "meaningful" contribution to society is cast as a large part of the problem.

The clearest dimension of this anti-welfarism is the idea that social assistance has fostered a culture of dependency. That is, rather than being a protective policy, the view is that welfare payments have come to be seen as a *right* that is ingratiatingly expected by the citizenry. Social assistance started out as a good idea: "To an unfortunate degree," argued Edward Newall, chair of the BCNI, "our whole philosophy as a country has changed. Once, Canadians concentrated on baking a bigger pie for all to share generously." But this generosity, in his opinion, has declined into selfishness and dependency: "Now, too often," Newall continued, "we quibble and quarrel over the size of our slice. A culture of entitlement is growing among us. This self-serving attitude is replacing the frontier spirit that built this country—a spirit based on self-reliance and community development" (1994: 9).

In a discussion on CBC's *Prime Time News* after the presentation of the Liberal budget in 1995, Brian Lee Crowley from the Atlantic Institute for Market Studies claimed that opinion polls in Atlantic Canada [he did not identify any specific polls] demonstrated that "people understand that things are no longer the way they once were, that government is no longer going to be there for them to depend on. And they have been waiting for someone to come along and offer them a plan to move from the kind of reliance on government that we've know for many years towards something different" (27 February 1995). The chief executive officer of BCE Inc., identifying an "obvious dichotomy between our fundamental values and our behaviour," drew the link between self-serving expectations and government prodigality even more bluntly: "We must abandon the notion of entitlements and champion thrift, self-reliance and character" (Wilson 1994: 3). As a final example, a *Globe and Mail* editorial extolling the debt cutting measures of the Newfoundland government of Clyde Wells, observes that Wells' "attempts to recast social assistance, to remove Newfoundland from the culture of dependence with a new form of income security, is also overdue" (1995: A10). These themes surfaced in Paul Martin's 1994 budget address: "The second challenge is to construct responsible social programs—not only so that they are affordable but more importantly so that they become builders of jobs—not barriers" (1994: 3).

On other occasions the leitmotif that welfare recipients simply abuse the system and invariably are indolent is manifest. A *Globe and Mail* editorial from the Ontario election of 1995 entitled "Who's really wacky here?" exposes the paper's underlying anti-welfarism when it compares Liberal leader Lyn McLeod and Premier Bob Rae to the Conservative leader Mike Harris by asking: "Is it radical to propose that the highest welfare rates in North America be lowered to 110 per cent of the Canadian average, and that able-bodied welfare recipients without young children be required to take training or do community-service jobs as a way of moving out of such dependence" (26 May 1995: A14). As a column by Gord Henderson in the *Windsor Star* reveals, these ideas are expressed occasionally with vitriol: "The party's over. Now it's time to clean up the horrendous mess left behind by the freeloaders, spendthrifts and do-gooders who've pushed this soft touch of a nation to the brink" (28 February 1995: A6).

Similar hostility towards social assistance programs was expressed in a segment on CBC's *Prime Time News* that addressed social policy reform. In the segment, a restaurant owner from the Bancroft area in Ontario calumniated against government welfare programs: "It is very difficult to understand how people can just sit at home and continually rape the system. . . . Why can't our government have people earn these monthly cheques instead of just letting them sit at home and continually waste their lives?" Of course, there is nothing unique about base polemics or perspectiveless class perspectives per se. Rather, what is interesting is that certain ideas illustrative of the time get conveyed through such ranting (in this case the link between indebtedness and "freeloaders" or the references to welfare abusers) while others do not get addressed.

## Conclusion

The discourse of fiscal crisis routinely draws an analogy between government finances and personal finances. Everyday experiences and understandings that are universally shared are used to render the notion of the debt crisis sensible. It is a very powerful device. The idea that the government is broke, that it is over-extending itself or that it is living beyond its means are easily understood. The fact that the analogy is groundless is irrelevant. It provides an avenue of comprehension, even if this comprehension is distorted.

The analogy is politically seductive or alluring. It creates support for the policy logic of the debt discourse. If the government is living beyond its means, then government spending must be cut, just as individuals would trim their financial outlays during tough times. The analogy, in effect, goes a considerable way towards cementing support for the neo-liberal policy agenda across class lines, especially among the working and marginalized classes. Thus, the reconstitution of class hegemony in the neo-liberal era is accomplished to a significant degree through the analogy of state fiscal management with personal financial management.

# Chapter Six

# The Suffocation of Politics

When we consider what, to use the words of the catechism, is the chief end of man, and what are the true necessaries and means of life, it appears as if men had deliberately chosen the common mode of living because they preferred it to any other. Yet they honestly think there is no choice left. But alert and healthy natures remember that the sun rose clear. It is never too late to give up our prejudices. No way of thinking or doing, however ancient, can be trusted without proof. What everybody echoes or in silence passes by as true to-day may turn out to be falsehood to-morrow, mere smoke of opinion, which some had trusted for a cloud that would sprinkle fertilising rain on their fields. (Henry David Thoreau, *Walden: or Life in the Woods*)

The latter quarter of the twentieth century has evinced great change. A new era of globally integrated trade and production, the second of the century, intensified from the 1970s onward. The century is ending in the same state as it began. Between these epochs of globalization, however, significant gains were achieved by the working classes in Europe and North America. The most visible manifestation of this, but certainly not the only manifestation, was the emergence of the welfare state. As the numerous but apparently forgotten histories of the working class in the first half of the twentieth century remind us, the welfare state was the product of worker resistance, protests, sit-ins, protracted strikes, pitched street battles and, on the other side, police repression, strategies of containment and co-optation, perceived threats to productivity and profits and, in the end, grudging concessions by capital. The unsightly or soiled nature of the struggle was lost on those numerous academic disquisitions outlining the functionalist nature of the welfare state, a position that has crept unforgivably into Marxist analysis as well.

As the twentieth century heads out Canadians have entered an age of rollback. The welfare state is being systematically dismantled. This development is part of a broader package of neo-liberal policies entering into the service of the Fordist transition. It is more telling to view this development as the evolution of the state in response to new strategies of accumulation in an era of precipitously declining profitability. The welfare state thwarted efforts to soften labour markets in Canada. Canada had to be made "more competitive" in an era of globalization.

There has been very little in the way of sustained responses to these trends in Canada. Why? Why are policies with such nasty human effects tolerated or even actively supported? Why does the opposition to these policies remain scattered and episodic? Obviously, a part of the answer lies in the logistical difficulties of co-ordinating oppositional groups and movements, that is, with consolidating social forces that stand in opposition to current trends. Still another answer might focus on the proliferation of social movements that seems to militate against the development of broader-based identities and political coalitions capable of uniting into a countervailing social force. Academia, of course, is partly responsible for these trends. As Michael Buroway points out, the tendency to celebrate the existence of new "social movements often stems from the *fact of* rather than the *reason for* their struggles" (Buroway 1985: 9, emphasis added)

In trying to account for the lack of opposition one might also draw attention to the lack of political leadership on behalf of the working classes and marginalized groups. Genuinely radical political parties that seek to undo capitalist productive life have a very low profile in Canada when compared with many European countries. The New Democratic parties at both the federal and provincial levels have proven to be incapable of providing a coherent response to the economic changes underway within Canada. The ease with which the social democratic alternative capitulated in the face of neo-liberalism attests to its muddled nature. In Ontario the NDP embraced accumulation strategies entirely consistent with the neo-liberal agenda. Indeed, the Ontario government became a vocal champion of fiscal restraint in view of growing debts. Federal New Democratic censuring of criticism of the Rae government in Ontario attested to the confusion and vacuity within the party. This is not the place to rehearse the argument against capitalist reformism. However, the pallid resistance of the NDP in Ontario was stunning even by the most sceptical standards.

Another answer might draw attention to the persuasive power of justifying terms that naturalize politically charged developments and numb (for the moment) the population to their harmful consequences. According to this narrative, the world has entered a new era of "globalization" in which Canada's competitive position must be restored and improved. Canada must respond to this new era of "global restructuring" to "avoid being left behind." Another idea regularly bandied about to justify neo-liberal policy is "job creation," an acutely ironic rationale in view of the fact that it manages to pass off profit-motivated behaviours as acts of goodwill or community kindness. On the government side these ideas are routinely trundled about to deregulate, privatize, cut, trim, streamline and improve the efficiency of the state. Curiously, journalists and political pundits have taken recently to summarizing the erosion of the so-called welfare state (itself a term that obfuscates the politics of its creation by suggesting that capitalism has an immanently benign side to it) with expressions such as "leaner and meaner governments" (a potentially prescient phrase if it metaphorizes the state as a boxer preparing for a big fight).

This study has advanced another explanation for the relatively unchallenged ascendency of the neo-liberal policy agenda. It argues that a primary reason for the rise of the neo-liberal agenda lies in the discourse of fiscal crisis. This discursive terrain fixes discussion and practices around the debt in a very specific way by calling attention to large yearly deficits and expanding government debts. In consequence, there is an emphasis on fiscal restraint to arrest debt expansion. In the end, federal deficits should be eliminated entirely and the process of discharging the debt must begin in earnest. If the federal and provincial governments fail in their bid to regain control over spending, then there will be a risk of government paralysis as its ability to raise money to fund programs weakens as it reaches the so-called debt wall.

It is the discourse of fiscal crisis that has nurtured the ascendency of the neo-liberal agenda in Canadian politics. Its discursive net comprises ideas that resonate within a broad cultural tapestry that has been constituted historically, especially with the evolution of capitalism. In particular, the debt discourse rests upon undergirding notions about individual responsibility and the nature of man and women, and draws on an intuitive sense of history. The following illustration demonstrates the individual, gendered and historical aspects of the discourse of fiscal crisis coalescing, as they often do, into one oration. Marshal Cohen, president of Molson Brewies Limited, draws upon all three aspects:

> One of the main problems is that the finance department now enjoys so little discretion. Most of the money is spent before the budget is written. This is one of those tragic budgets where *the government has slashed it wrists and bled all over the floor* to make whatever

cuts they can, but the business community will dismiss it as nothing much. Therefore, we need a politician who will say "Look, *the cupboard is bare*, there is no more money for welfare payments, no more funds for most of the things governments do. . . ." This issue isn't going to be resolved merely by cutting out universality. That is only the beginning; that is only *the painless stuff*. It simply won't be enough to take money away from the *people who don't need it*. You are going to have to get at the people who really need it as well. That is not so much a question of political courage as having *the stomach to do it*, because it is going to be *very, very painful*. (1989: 48, emphasis added)

The above reference to bare cupboards reflects the tendency to analogize the debt with everyone's personal financial experiences, an especially effective analogy as personal indebtedness has been growing. At the same time, the linking of government spending with unworthy recipients —"people who don't need it"—plugs the debt discourse into anti-*dirigiste* notions regarding the state. Within this atmosphere the state moves from *being there* for people to *being preyed upon* by indolent scavengers and cheats. Snitch lines for reporting welfare abuse, for example, get justified as a legitimate deficit reduction strategy.

While these aspects of the discourse are unconscionable, its most disturbing dimension lies in its gendered and historical intersections. The discourse of fiscal crisis is undergirded by patriarchal consciousness. In particular, the debt discourse is constituted with the language of resolve and courage, a fear of loss of control, representations of a purely abstract quality, claims of being exclusively reasonable and the voice of authority. Through the mechanisms of patriarchal consciousness the debt discourse figuratively becomes a sealed discourse associated with reasonableness and sensibility. Therein lies much of its power. Any political position that advocates increases in government spending are automatically identified as unreasonable. Advocacy in general is deemed to be socially irresponsible in an era of restraint. Persistent advocacy and critiques of neo-liberal strategies, therefore, inevitably lead to public ridicule. There is a growing tendency to dismiss such groups as "special interests." Political debate tends to get subordinated to the exigencies of debt reduction. The most relevant political question has become "How much?" rather than "Why?" The discourse of fiscal crisis, therefore, is a politics of suffocation. Criticism is silenced. To be heard, one must jettison a politics of advocacy. And the realm of political contestation understood as comprising competing visions of society vanishes altogether.

Consequently, a basic paradox emerges in the context of the debt crisis/ neo-liberal nexus. Neo-liberal policies exacerbate the social dislocations and human hardships characteristic of capitalist society. At the same time, this nexus undermines those groups attempting to address issues such as the intensification of poverty or declining health care. As things get worse, in short, the opportunities to deal with them effectively are narrowed. It is a struggle just *to be heard* at a time when it is most necessary for oppositional groups to have a voice. Advocacy groups are thrown onto the defensive for even venting the concerns of different social constituencies, even those publicly recognized victims of "belt-tightening." Ironically, they are sometimes depicted as the cause of the social injury they seek to repair. This is especially evident in the idea that they cultivate a culture of reliance—a criticism sometimes made of food banks, for example. In the climate of funding restraint they also are forced to rationalize their operations, tighten eligibility, expand their fundraising efforts and flirt with ideas such as user fees or service charges. In general, advocacy groups are subjected to intensified public scrutiny and criticism. Progressive social groups are forced into competition with one another as funding sources dry up, with the effect of decreasing political resistance at a time when it is most needed.

The debt discourse also intersects with ideas about decaying historical trajectories. The debt is represented as the product of profligacy. History has been side-tracked by prodigality and irresponsibility. Metaphors of bodily disease and mental degeneration are employed to underscore the errancy of the contemporary period. The sayers of the crisis, therefore, are akin to the chorus in a Greek tragedy, dispensing guidance and admonishing the (political) players in the face of immoderation and irresponsibility.

The real tragedy within this tragic narrative, however, arises from the fact that it is the sayers of the crisis who are confused and immoderate. The sayers of the crisis are not the voice of wisdom and balanced judgement. Rather, their interests are mercenary and lacking in human perspective. As such, they factor into the class assault underway in Canada. Unlike the protracted strikes and pitched street battles associated with a recalcitrant working class, this assault is being waged by the capitalist class. Their target is the working classes, the under-employed, the unemployed and the marginalized poor. Their goal is to lower production costs, especially by depressing wages.

Only an extraneous political critique can cut through the self-replicating logic and circularity of the discourse of fiscal crisis. No organic political movement with this capacity is visible on the horizon. No mass-based political movement in Canadian society shows even a hint of developing a coherent response capable of cutting through the neo-liberal agenda. It is perhaps the most sobering commentary on the genuine Canadian left that the Natural Law Party receives more attention than any bonafide socialist or communist group. Sustained critiques of capitalism, in short, are not conspicuous by their absence. But they are desperately needed.

# REFERENCES

Aglietta, M. 1979. *A Theory of Capitalist Regulation: The US Experience*. London: New Left Books.

Albo, Gregory. 1994. "'Competitive Austerity' and the Impasse of Capitalist Employment Policy." *Socialist Register 1994*. London: Merlin.

Armstrong, Pat. 1995. "Unravelling the Social Safety Net." In Janine Brodie, ed., *Women and Canadian Public Policy*. Toronto: Harcourt, Brace and Jovanovich.

Bakker, Isabella. 1995. "The Politics of Scarcity: Deficits and the Debt." In M. Whittington and G. Williams, eds., *Canadian Politics in the 1990s*. Scarborough: Nelson.

Banting, Keith. 1986. "Images of the Modern State." In Keith Banting, ed., *State and Society: Canada, A Comparative Perspective*. Toronto: University of Toronto Press.

Bienefield, F. and Duncan Cameron. n.d. *Bleeding the Patient: The Debt/ Deficit Hoax Exposed*. Ottawa: Canadian Centre for Policy Alternatives.

Bina, Cyrus and Behzad Yaghmaian. 1991. "Postwar Global Accumulation and the Transnationalization of Capital." *Capital and Class* 43 (Spring): 107–30.

Blythe, Scott, Glenn Allen, Luke Fisher and Nancy Wood. 1993. "Squeezing Ottawa: Everyone Promises to Reduce the Deficit, But There Are Few Specifics." *Maclean's* 106, 18 (10 May): 10–12.

Braverman, Harry. 1974. *Labour and Monopoly Capital: The Degradation of Work in the Twentieth Century*. New York: Monthly Review.

Brenner, Robert and Mark Glick. 1991. "The Regulation Approach: Theory and History." *New Left Review* 188 (July/August): 45–119.

Bruce, Neil and Douglas D. Purvis. 1984. "Evaluating the Deficit: The Case for Budget Cuts." Toronto: C.D. Howe Institute.

Buroway, Michael. 1985. *The Politics of Production*. London: Verso.

Business Council on National Issues. 1994. "A Ten Point Growth and

Employment Strategy for Canada." Ottawa: Business Council on National Issues.

C. D. Howe Institute. 1994. *Building a Constituency for Deficit Reduction.* Toronto: C. D. Howe Institute.

Cameron, Duncan. 1989. "Political Discourse in the Eighties." In Alain Gagnon and Brian Tanguay eds., *Canadian Parties in Transition: Discourse, Organization and Representation.* Scarborough: Nelson.

Canadian Chamber of Commerce. n.d. "If We Care About People . . . " Canadian Chamber of Commerce.

CHO!CES. 1995. *Alternative Federal Budget 1995.* Winnipeg: CHO!CES.

Chorney, Harold, John Hotson, Mario Secareccia and Ed Finn. 1992. *"The Deficit Made Me Do It!": The Myths About Government Debt.* Ottawa: Canadian Centre for Policy Alternatives.

Cox, Robert W. 1987. *Production, Power and World Order: Social Forces in the Making of History.* New York: Columbia University.

———. 1992. "Global Perestroika." In Ralph Miliband and Leo Panitch, eds., *New World Order? The Socialist Register 1992.* London: Merlin.

d'Aquino, Thomas P. 1986. Address to Rotary Club. (20 January). Ottawa.

———. 1989. "Deficits and the National Debt. The Silent Threat to Canada's Prosperity." Address to the Rotary Club, Ballroom, Chateau Laurier, 23 February. Ottawa: Business Council on National Issues.

———. 1994. *Growth, Employment and Fiscal Responsibility.* Ottawa: Business Council on National Issues.

Dehli, Kari. 1993. "Subject to the New Global Economy: Power and Positioning in Ontario Labour Market Policy Formation." *Studies in Political Economy* 41 (Summer): 83–110.

Duménil, Gérard, Mark Glick and José Rangel. 1985. "The Tendency of the Rate of Profit to Fall in the United States." *Contemporary Marxism* 11 (Fall): 138–52.

Ernst, Alan. 1992. "From Liberal Continentalism to Neoconservatism: North American Free Trade and the Politics of the C.D. Howe Institute." *Studies in Political Economy* 39 (Autumn): 109–40.

Friedmann, Harriet. 1991. "New Wines, New Bottles: The Regulation of Capital on a World Scale." *Studies in Political Economy* 36 (Fall): 9–42.

Fukuyama, Francis. 1992. *The End of History and the Last Man.* New York: Free Press.

Gallup Poll. 1995. "Public Spit on Deficit-Unemployment Tradeoff." *The Gallop Poll* 55, 18 (27 February).

Glynn, Andrew and Bob Sutcliffe. 1992. "Global But Leaderless? The New Capitalist Order." *The Socialist Register 1992.* London: Merlin.

Gramsci, Antonio. 1971. *Prison Notebooks.* New York: International Publishers.

Gray, Grattan. 1990. "Social Policy by Stealth." *Policy Options* 11, 2 (March): 17–29.

Grinspun, Ricardo and Robert Kreklewich. 1994. "Consolidating Neo-liberal Reforms: 'Free Trade as a Conditioning Framework.'" *Studies in Political Economy* 43 (Spring): 33–61.

Hall, Stuart. 1979. "The Great Moving Right Show." *Marxism Today* 23, 1 (January).

———. 1983. "Whistling in the Void." *New Socialist* 11 (May/June): 8–12.

Harris, Richard. 1993. *Deficits and Debt in the Canadian Economy.* Kingston: John Deutsch Institute for the Study of Economic Policy, Queen's University.

———. 1994. "The Public Debt and the Social Policy Round." In Richard G. Harris, John Richards, David M. Brown and John McCallum, *Paying Our Way: The Welfare State in Hard Times.* Toronto: C.D. Howe Institute.

Harvey, David. 1989. *The Condition of Postmodernity.* Oxford: Basil Blackwell.

Jenson, Jane. 1991. "All the World's a Stage: Ideas, Spaces and Times in Canadian Political Economy." *Studies in Political Economy* 36 (Fall): 43–72.

Jessop, Bob. 1993. "Towards a Schumpeterian Workfare State? Preliminary Remarks on Post-Fordist Political Economy." *Studies in Political Economy* 40 (Spring): 7–39.

Keller, Evelyn Fox. 1985. *Reflections on Gender and Science.* New Haven: Yale University.

Laidler, David E.W. and William B.P. Robson. 1995. "Don't Break the Bank! The Role of Monetary Policy in Deficit Reduction." *C.D. Howe Institute Commentary* 66 (February).

Langille, David. 1987. "The Business Council on National Issues and the Canadian State." *Studies in Political Economy* 24 (Autumn): 41–85.

Lash, Scott and John Urry. 1987. *The End of Organized Capitalism.* Cambridge. Polity Press.

Lipietz, A. 1986. "New Tendencies in the International Division of Labour: Regimes of Accumulation and Modes of Regulation." In A. Scott and M. Storper, eds., *Production, Work, Territory: The Geographical Anatomy of Industrial Capitalism.* London: Allen and Unwin.

Macdonald, Laura. 1995. "Canada and the 'New World Order.'" In M. Whittington and G. Williams, eds., *Canadian Politics in the 1990s.* Scarborough: Nelson.

Magdoff, Harry. 1992. "Globalisation—To What End?" *The Socialist Register 1992.* London: Merlin.

Martin, Paul. 22 February 1994. *Budget Speech.* Ottawa: Department of

Finance.

———. 27 February 1995. *Budget Speech*. Ottawa: Department of Finance.

Marx, Karl. 1976. *The German Ideology*. Moscow: Progress.

Mazankowski, Don. 25 February 1992. *The Budget 1992*. Ottawa: Department of Finance.

———. 26 April 1993. *The Budget 1993*. Ottawa: Department of Finance.

McMurdy, Deidre. 1993. "The Debt Beats." *Maclean's* 106, 13 (29 March): 26–8.

McQuaig, Linda. 1993. *The Wealthy Banker's Wife*. Toronto: Penguin.

———. 1995. *Shooting the Hippo: Death by Deficit and Other Canadian Myths*. Toronto: Viking.

National Council of Welfare. 1995. *Poverty Profile 1993: A Report by the National Council of Welfare*. Ottawa: Ministry of Supply and Services.

Newall, J. Edward. 1994. "Canada's Future: Facing Up to Our Responsibility." Ottawa: Business Council on National Issues.

Newman, Peter C. 1989. "A Pessimistic and Enraging Budget." *Maclean's* (8 May).

———. 1991. "Wilson's Vain Struggle with a Killer Debt." *Maclean's* 104, 9 (4 March): 46.

Ornstein, Michael. 1985. "Canadian Capital and the Canadian State: Ideology in an Era of Crisis." In R.J. Brym, ed., *The Structure of the Canadian Capitalist Class*. Toronto: Garamond.

Panitch, Leo. 1987. "Capitalist Restructuring and Labour Strategies." *Studies in Political Economy* 24 (Autumn): 131-49.

———. 1994. "Globalization and the State." *Socialist Register 1994*. London: Merlin.

Picciotto, Sol. 1991. "The Internationalisation of the State." *Capital and Class* 43 (Spring): 43–63.

Reform Party of Canada. 1993. *Stop Digging!: A Presentation of the Reform Party's Plan to Reduce the Federal Deficit to Zero in Three Years*. Ottawa: Reform Party of Canada.

Reuber, Grant. 1980. *Canada's Political Economy: Current Issues*. Toronto: McGraw-Hill Ryerson.

Rice, James. 1993. "Lowering the Safety Net and Weakening the Bonds of Nationhood: Social Policy in the Mulroney Years." In Susan Phillips, ed., *How Ottawa Spends, 1993–94*. Ottawa: Carleton University Press.

Richards, John. 1994. "The Study in Brief." In Richard G. Harris, John Richards, David M. Brown and John McCallum, *Paying Our Way: The Welfare State in Hard Times*. Toronto: C.D. Howe Institute.

Richardson, Robin. 1994. "Inside Canada's Government Debt Problem and the Way Out." *Fraser Forum*.

Rinehart, James W. 1987. *The Tyranny of Work: Alienation and the Labour*

*Process.* Toronto: Harcourt, Brace and Jovanovich.

Robson, William B.P. 1993. "Don't Bet on the Bank: Monetary Policy and Canada's Growing Foreign Debt." *C.D. Howe Institute Commentary* 47 (May).

———. 1994. "Digging Holes and Hitting Walls: Canada's Fiscal Prospects in the Mid-1990s." *C.D. Howe Institute Commentary* 56 (January).

Ross, D., E.R. Shillington and C. Lockhead. 1994. *The Canadian Fact Book on Poverty.* Ottawa: Canadian Council on Social Development.

Ruddick, Sara. 1989. *Maternal Thinking: Toward a Politics of Peace.* New York: Ballantine.

Taylor, Charles. 1985. "Interpretation and the Sciences of Man." In P.A. French, T.E. Uehling Jr. and H.K. Wettstein, eds., *Philosophy and the Human Sciences.* New York: Cambridge University Press.

Taylor, F.W. 1919. *The Principles of Scientific Management.* New York: Harper and Brothers.

Thoreau, Henry David. n.d. *Walden: or Life in the Woods.* Norwalk, CT: The Easton Press.

Walkom, Thomas. 1994. *Rae Days: The Rise and Follies of the NDP.* Toronto: Key Porter.

Weir, Lorna. 1993. "Limitations of New Social Movement Analysis." *Studies in Political Economy* 40 (Spring): 73–102.

Wilson, L.R. 1994. "Three Wishes for Canada." *Canadian Business Leaders Speak.* Ottawa: Business Council on National Issues.

Wilson, Michael. 26 February 1986. *The Budget.* Ottawa: Department of Finance.

———. 27 April 1989. *The Budget.* Ottawa: Department of Finance.

———. 20 February 1990. *The Budget.* Ottawa: Department of Finance.

———. 26 February 1991. *The Budget.* Ottawa: Department of Finance.

Wolfe, David. 1985. "The Politics of the Deficit." In Bruce Doern, ed., *The Politics of Economic Policy.* Toronto: University of Toronto Press.

# Related titles
# from Fernwood Publishing

## INVISIBLE GIANT
## Cargill and its Transnational Strategies
*Brewster Kneen*

Cargill is the epitome of a transnational corporation—the largest private corporation in North America, and possibly in the world, it trades in all agricultural commodities and produces and processes a great many of them.

Cargill is both wealthy and influential, and there are few national economies unaffected by its activities. Yet it remains largely invisible to most people and accountable to no one. Using Cargill as the focus for his study, Kneen clearly illustrates the philosophy and practice of transnational corporations (TNCs); what they are and what they do. Kneen describes and analyses Cargill's global activities, its ability to shape national policies worldwide, its strategies, and the implications of these strategies for all of us.

*"The result of (Kneen's) sleuthing is a remarkable amount of information which is frightening but ultimately empowering." —Hariett Friedman, U. of Toronto*

Co-published witih Pluto Press   paper   232 pp   ISBN 1 895686 56 3   $24.95

## APOSTLES OF GREED
## Capitalism and the Myth of the Individual in the Market
*Allan Engler*

"Provides a readable history of the eighteenth century origins of the 'myth of the individual in the market,' traces subsequent modifications of this idea, and details its contemporary revival. But Engler not only provides a genealogy, he provides a pungent convincing critique of capitalism's holiest of holy relics. Chapters on corporate oligopoly, corporate hierarchy, the concentrated political power of the corporate oligarchy, and its globalization undermine utterly the arbitrary assumptions on which competitive market theory is founded. . . Like other religious relics, once removed from its ritual setting, the mythology of the individual in the market looks so tawdry and illogical one wonders how it became so potent."

*—Libby Davis, Pacific Current*

Co-published with Pluto Press   paper   187 pp   ISBN 1 895686 53 9   $24.95

## INTERNATIONAL POLITICAL ECONOMY
## Understanding Global Disorder
*Björn Hettne ed.*

In this book, some of the most emminent theorists grapple with the difficult questions involved in developing appropriate theoretical tools in order to understand the rapidly changing, inter-connected structures of international relations and the global eocnomy, and the multiple new sources of instability, integration and inequality. One of the central themes to emerge is the disjuncture between the way in which the world is organized politically (with the sovereign state still the principal actor) and its economic organization (characterized by more and more integration via the market and international institutions for cross-border cooperation).

This collection provides an essential introduction to the innovative thinking that is rapidly transforming the frontiers of international political economy as a discipline.
Contributors: Robert Cox, Stephen Gill, Björn Hettne, Kees van der Pijl, James Rosenau, Yoshikazu Sakamoto.

Co-published with Zed Books   paper   152pp   ISBN 1 895686 58 X   $19.95

## SOMETHING'S WRONG SOMEWHERE
## Globalization, Community and the Moral Economy
## of the Farm Crisis
*Christopher Lind*

" . . . offers a refreshingly human perspective on an issue that has been dominated for too long by purely economic considerations. . . . Lind's book speaks to the long history of unique values and strength of purpose that helped create a special place in rural Canada, and offers renewed hope that it can be saved." —*Verne Clemence, The Star Phoenix, Saskatoon.*

"Recalling the fascinating history of rural protests in seventeenth to nineteenth century England, he argues that today's crisis has as much to do with morals and ethics as with economics." —*Kim Cariou, People's Voice, Vancouver.*

Paper  100pp   ISBN 1 895686 50 4   $12.95

## DISMANTLING A NATION
## Canada and the New World Order
*Stephen McBride and John Shields*

All the aspects of the neo-conservative policy matrix—privatization,deregulation, nafta, the obsession with deficits, attacks on collective bargaining, the cutbacks to social programs, the weakening of federal powers—are carefully analyzed as elements of a political project that will have disasterous consequences for most Canadians and for Canada as a nation. This book is truly essential reading for those who care about Canada's future." —*William K. Carroll, Sociology, Universit of Victoria*

Contents: Neo-Conservatism in Canada: Importing a Foriegn Model • Dismantlin the Keynesian Welfare State • The Neo-Conservative Constitutional Agenda • Embedding the Neo-Conservative Doctrine: The Canadian Political Economy and Continental Free Trade • A Nation Dismantled: The Challenge of Canadian Politic in the Post-Mulroney Era

Paper   208 pp   ISBN 1 895686 14 8   $19.95


## POWER AND RESISTANCE
## Critical Thinking about Social Issues in Canada
*Les Samuelson ed.*

In this text/reader the individual authors argue that understanding injustice means revealing the various mechanisms through which dominant groups attempt to express and reproduce their social/economic and political control. On the other sid of this coin are the affected groups who attempt to resist and change the suffering they are forced to endure. Hierarchies of class/gender and race and the manner in which they are played out on the contested terrain of the state are central organizir principles in understanding what we often call "social problems."

Contributors: Samuelson • Battle • Knuttila • Satzewich • Waldrom • Ursel • Greschner • McDaniel • Samuelson •   Kinsman • Grant • Morrow • Bolaria • Klos • McBride • Shields • Satzewich

Paper   294 pp   ISBN 1 895686 34 2   $24.95